✤ Bread of Angels

Jean,
I hope you enjoy her words!

Bruce

Vesty 2013

BARBARA BROWN TAYLOR

Bread of Angels

A COWLEY PUBLICATIONS BOOK

ROWMAN & LITTLEFIELD PUBLISHERS, INC.
Lanham, Chicago, New York, Toronto, and Plymouth, UK

A COWLEY PUBLICATIONS BOOK

ROWMAN & LITTLEFIELD PUBLISHERS, INC.

Published in the United States of America
by Rowman & Littlefield Publishers, Inc.
A wholly owned subsidary of The Rowman & Littlefield Publishing Group, Inc.
4501 Forbes Boulevard, Suite 200, Lanham, Maryland 20706
www.rowmanlittlefield.com

Estover Road
Plymouth PL6 7PY
United Kingdom

Distributed by National Book Network

British Library Cataloguing in Publication Information Available

Library of Congress Cataloging-in-Publication Data

Taylor, Barbara Brown.
  Bread of angels / Barbara Brown Taylor
    p. cm.
  ISBN-10: 1-56101-142-8   ISBN-13: 978-1-56101-142-1
  1. Episcopal Church—Sermons. 2. Sermons. American.   I. Title.
BX5937.T28B74 1997
252'.0373—dc21   97-19224

Cover design: Brad Norr Design
Interior design: Wendy Holdman

Printed in the United States of America

For my other mother
Fannie Belle Taylor

Contents

Preface

TRUE WINE CONNOISSEURS CAN TAKE A SIP OF WINE and tell you all about the grape: what kind of soil it grew in, in what part of the world, under what weather conditions. All the information is right there on the tongue for those who know how to read it. In the same way, I suppose, a sermon bears the marks of its origins. Properly done, it is a particular word to a particular people at a particular moment in time. The language, the images, and the concerns all reveal a congregation as well as a preacher, which makes those who listen to a sermon collaborators in the creation of it.

In the case of the sermons that follow, my collaborators are four hundred souls who live in the foothills of north Georgia and call themselves Grace-Calvary Church. They include mechanics, professors, farmers, and homemakers, with all the usual hopes and fears. They want to know God. They are afraid to know God. They worry about their children. They try to live right. They get in fights. They make up. They pray together. They are the church.

God's word is their and my daily bread. Whether it comes to us straight off the page or embodied in the events of our days, we mean to receive it as manna from heaven, the sometimes strange food upon which our lives depend. If you too are subject to the usual hopes and fears, I hope you find some bread here. You may thank the angels if you do.

Bread of Angels

One

Glory Doors

---

*As he came down from the mountain with the two tablets of the
covenant in his hand, Moses did not know that the skin of his
face shone because he had been talking with God.*

EXODUS 34:29

I F YOU STUDIED ART HISTORY IN SCHOOL, YOU MAY
have come across the famous statue of Moses by Michelangelo.
Carved out of pure white marble, he is all flowing beard and bil-
lowing robes, with the two tablets of the law cradled in his arms
and two distinct horns coming out of his head. If you are not
ready for the horns they can be quite a shock, since they make
him look as much like a devil as a prophet, but a passage from
the book of Exodus holds the clue.

> When Aaron and all the Israelites saw Moses, the skin
> of his face was shining, and they were afraid to come
> near him. (Exodus 34:30)

It turns out that the Hebrew word for "shining," *karan*, is identi-
cal to the word for "horn," *keren*. The only difference is in the
vowels, which were not spelled out in ancient Hebrew, so some
interpreters, including Michelangelo, decided that Moses' face
had sprouted horns, not light, during his encounter with God.

But everyone agreed that something major had happened to him. He had spent forty days on Mount Sinai with the Lord God Almighty, receiving the ten commandments for the second time. While he was up there, he asked to see God's glory and God obliged, wedging Moses into the cleft of a rock and passing by so that Moses saw God's back. It was more than any human being had ever been allowed to see before.

No one could look upon God's face and live. It would suck the breath right out of you. It would dissolve all your bones and turn your flesh to ash, vaporizing you into pure spirit on the spot. Or that is what people supposed. No one knew for sure because it had never happened, thanks to the infinite mercy of God.

God protected people from the full impact of deity, the same way Moses was protected. God shielded people, by hiding inside an envelope of light that was the only thing most people could see. Sometimes it looked to them like a pillar of cloud or fire, sometimes like a volcano, but no one ever mistook it for a natural phenomenon. It was brighter than anything on earth, like a doorway to some other world, and though the door remained closed most of the time, even the shafts of light that got through the cracks could blind anyone silly enough to look right at them.

The light was the sure sign of God's presence on earth, and for lack of a better word people began to call it God's glory. When they were worshiping together and the tent where they met filled up with light, they said it was the glory of the Lord. Sometimes it got so thick they could not see each other. All they could see was a dazzling brightness that left stars in their eyes long after it was over, but no matter how strong it was, how palpable, God remained hidden inside of it. They could not see God. They could only see God's glory, which was all that most of them could bear.

But Moses saw more. Moses saw God's back, and it was such a strong dose of glory that some of it rubbed off on him. When he came down the mountain the skin of his face was shining, and people were afraid of him. They would not come near him, until finally he persuaded his brother Aaron and some of the other leaders to tiptoe up to him and hear what he had to say. When the Israelites saw that no one dropped dead, they dared to approach him too and Moses delivered the commandments to them for the second time.

When Moses finished speaking to them he put a veil on his face (a handkerchief, maybe, or a scarf he borrowed from his sister Miriam?) because he did not want to scare them. Either that or he was tired of people staring at him. But whenever Moses went to speak with God or came back to tell the people what God had said, he removed the veil so everyone could see his shining face. They might not be able to see God directly, but they could see God's glory reflected in Moses. God had given them someone they could look at and listen to, someone who walked around in his own personal spotlight.

The same thing happened to Jesus a thousand years later. His mountain was in Israel, not Egypt, but it was clearly the same glory that enveloped him. As three of his disciples watched him pray, his face changed. It got whiter and brighter until his whole body was as blinding as a lightning bolt that would not go out. It just stayed on him, crackling with power, while Moses and Elijah appeared inside the glory with him. They spoke of his departure, Luke says. They spoke of his death inside that blazing circle, and even that did not make the light go out.

I often wonder if things might have gone better for him if his glory had lasted longer, as Moses' did. Jesus never had to wear a veil. By the time he came down from the mountain his face was back to normal. No one was particularly afraid of him, at least not in the right way. They were afraid of him in the wrong way—afraid enough to kill him. Could they have done that, do you think, if his face had been shining? It is almost as if God took the glory one step further with Jesus, taking it off his face and tucking it inside him. God hid it there, to see if people could still discern the glory without the visual aid. Still, what happened on the mountain must have helped Jesus. It must have helped him to know what was inside him, even if it was not always visible.

The church's word for what happened to Moses and Jesus is *transfiguration*. While people who knew them both very well watched, they were changed into beings of light, as if their skin had become transparent for a moment and what had been inside them all along shone through for everyone to see. It was not anything either of them did. They did not change. They were changed, by the God whose glory transfigures everyone it touches. It is light that cannot be captured or controlled, any more than God can be. It can only be experienced, in ourselves or in another. It can only be believed.

What we are asked to believe is that at certain breakthrough moments in time, the glory of God is certifiably visible. A veil is necessary. Disciples' eyes water from the glare. The bright envelope of God's presence draws near and people can actually see it for themselves, a radiance that burns itself into the back of their eyelids so that they never forget. We are asked to believe that, and sometimes I think that setting out to see that glory is the only thing worth doing in life.

But seeing it may not be the most important thing because we are also asked to believe in it when we cannot see it, when we are stuck in dark rooms we do not even know the contours of and we cannot find the light. In situations like that, all we have are the stories. Stories are strong, once you decide to believe in them. They can change your life, and if we believe in these two about Moses and Jesus, then we live in a different world from people who do not.

We live in a world where glory is possible, where light may break through any moment. We believe in what we can see, but we believe in more than that. Earth and flesh, comfort and sorrow, are terribly important to us, but they are not elemental. The world is not made out of them. The world is made out of light, which is straining against the skin of the world even as we speak. You never know when a face may begin to shine, including your own, but even when we cannot see the light, we believe in it, because we have heard the stories. We know that God's glory is pulsing just beneath the surface of things, with power to transfigure the darkest of our days.

I say "we believe," but of course I also mean "we want to believe," which is the moving paradox of faith. Every day we count on things we cannot see to hold us when we fall. We entrust the weight of our lives to things we cannot prove. By the power of our beliefs, we choose what kind of world we will live in—a porous world, full of glory doors leaking light, or a flat world where everything is exactly what it seems. I leave you with the stories, to make up your own minds.

Two

Bread of Angels

When the layer of dew lifted, there on the surface of the wilderness was a fine flaky substance, as fine as frost on the ground. When the Israelites saw it, they said to one another, "What is it?" For they did not know what it was.

EXODUS 16:14–15

AS A CHILD OF THE SOUTH, I ATE GRITS FOR YEARS without knowing what they were. I ate cheese grits, buttered grits, grits with pieces of crisp bacon stirred in—and not instant grits, either, but slow-cooking grits, the kind that take twenty minutes to make and end up swimming in their own gravy. Finally, when I was about twelve, I asked a friend of mine if he knew what they were. "The truth?" he said, grinning wickedly. "You really want to know the truth?"

He told me that grits were small bugs that lived in colonies on the surface of fresh-water lakes, like algae, and at the end of every summer they were harvested, shelled, and dried in the sun so that you could not even tell they ever had legs on them. "Mmmm-mmmm," he concluded, as my stomach drew itself into a ball.

So whenever I hear about manna, I think of grits. They are both fine, flaky things that are absolutely no good as leftovers. "Each day the people shall go out and gather enough for that day," God told Moses. One day's worth, no more, because manna would not keep. If the people tried to hoard it, it spoiled overnight. In the morning it stank and crawled with worms. When the sun got hot, it melted. So their limit was two quarts of manna per day per person.

The only exception was the sabbath. Since God meant the people to rest on that day, there was no manna to be found. God let them gather twice as much as they needed the day before and on that one day a week it lasted two days instead of one. So the people rested on the seventh day and the next day they were back at it again, living one day at a time by the providence of almighty God.

This lasted forty years, or fourteen thousand six hundred days. Manna was the Israelites' food in the wilderness. They ate raw manna, boiled manna, baked manna, ground manna. It was how they survived until they came into the land of Canaan, so that manna became for them the symbol of God's very practical, physical care for them. Long after their sojourn in the desert was over, they remembered their manna meals. At God's command, they kept two quarts of it in a jar right by the tablets of the law as an everlasting reminder of their dependence on God, who gave them each day their daily bread.

There has been a good bit of speculation over the years about exactly what manna was. The Bible says it was "like coriander seed, white, and the taste of it was like wafers made with honey" (Exodus 16:31). The name comes from the Hebrew *man hu*—which means "What is it?"—but if you go to the Sinai peninsula it will not stay a mystery very long. The Bedouin who live there still gather it and bake it into bread, which they still call manna. The flakes themselves come from plant lice that feed on the local tamarisk trees. Because the sap is poor in nitrogen, the bugs have to eat a lot of it in order to live. They excrete the extra in a yellowish-white flake or ball of juice from the tree that is rich in carbohydrates and sugars. It decays quickly and attracts ants, so a daily portion is the most anyone gathers. Does that sound familiar?

Some believers reject this explanation because they think it takes away from the miracle of manna, but I wonder about that. Does manna have to come out of nowhere in order to qualify as a miracle? Or is the miracle that God heard the complaining of hungry people and fed them with bug juice—with food it would never have occurred to them to eat? Or to put it another way, what makes something bread from heaven? Is it the thing itself or the one who sends it?

How you answer those questions has a lot to do with how you sense God's presence in your life. If your manna has to drop straight out of heaven looking like a perfect loaf of butter-crust bread, then chances are you are going to go hungry a lot. When you do not get the miracle you are praying for, you are going to think that God is ignoring you or punishing you or—worse yet—that God is not there. You are going to start comparing yourself to other people and wondering why they seem to have more to eat than you do, and you may start complaining to heaven about that. Meanwhile, you are going to miss a lot of other things God is doing for you because they are too ordinary—like bug juice—or too transitory—like manna, that fine, flaky substance that melted as soon as the sun got hot.

If, on the other hand, you are willing to look at everything that comes to you as coming to you from God, then there will be no end to the manna in your life. A can of beans will be manna. Grits will be manna. Bug juice will be manna. Nothing will be too ordinary or too transitory to remind you of God. When you go to bed hungry and you wake up to find a fine, flaky substance on the ground, you will say, "What is it?" and when someone says, "It is the bread that the Lord has given you to eat," you will believe it. You will say "Thanks be to God," and start trying to figure out how to eat the stuff.

Because it is not what it is that counts but who sent it, and the miracle is that God is always sending us something to eat. Day by day, God is made known to us in the simple things that sustain our lives—some bread, some love, some breath, some wine—all those absolutely essential things that are here today and gone tomorrow. Everything else is gravy, but it is easy to forget that. Come to my house and I will show you a pantry crammed with canned food and a refrigerator so full that the green beans fall out every time I open the door. It is my manna-insurance, just in case God does not come through. At least I know who gave it to me, so perhaps that makes it manna too.

Either way, I am on manna alert, and I know that it is about more than food. After Jesus fed the five thousand in their wilderness, they stuck to him like glue. The miracle of the loaves reminded them of the manna stories they had heard and they thought they had their very own Moses to work wonders for them. Testing their premise, they asked Jesus to prove himself by producing bread from heaven on the spot. They wanted the butter-crust loaves, but he knew they needed more than that, so he gave them himself instead—which, believe me, sounded like bug juice to some of them.

They wanted miracle food to eat, not a relationship with this ordinary looking man. He honored their hunger even as he corrected them. It was not Moses who gave it to them, he explained. It was God who gave it and God who gives the true bread from heaven, the bread that gives life to the world. "Give us this bread always," they said, and that is when he let them know that they were looking at it. "I am the bread of life," he told them. Jesus is God's manna in the wilderness, the one who reminds us day by day that we live because God provides not what we want, necessarily, but exactly what we need: some bread, some love, some breath, some wine, a relationship with this ordinary looking man, who comes from heaven to bring life to the world.

Three

You Are the Man

~

When the wife of Uriah heard that her husband was dead,
she made lamentation for him. When the mourning was over,
David sent and brought her to his house, and she became his
wife, and bore him a son.

2 SAMUEL 11:26–27

KING DAVID WAS ONE OF THE GREATEST HEROES
Israel ever had. He was handsome, the Bible says, ruddy, with
beautiful eyes. He was a fearless fighter, even in his youth, when
he faced Goliath without a single piece of armor on and brought
him—thump—to the ground with a river rock. He went on to
become a brilliant military strategist and city planner. Jerusalem
was his idea. It was he who made it the capital of Israel and united
the kingdom under his rule. He was artistic too, a musician and
a composer of psalms. When David played his lyre, everybody's
headaches went away and smiles stole over their faces.

He was God's anointed one, and in the first book of Kings
you can read how he went down in history:

David did what was right in the sight of the Lord, and
did not turn aside from anything that he commanded
him all the days of his life, except in the matter of Uriah
the Hittite. (I Kings 15:5)

Uriah who? Uriah the Hittite. Loyal soldier in David's army. Unfortunate husband of the beautiful Bathsheba, whom David happened to see bathing one day while he was walking on the roof of his house. He took one look at her and he had to have her. He sent his messengers to bring her to him and before long she sent him back a message of her own. "I am pregnant," she told him, and David's strategical mind went into high gear.

The first thing he tried was a cover-up. If he could get Uriah and Bathsheba to spend a romantic weekend together, Uriah might believe the child was his own. The only problem was that Uriah was out of town fighting a battle and like all other soldiers he was sworn to celibacy until the fight was over. David ordered him back to Jerusalem and told him to go see his wife, but Uriah refused. The same thing happened the next day, so the day after that David invited Uriah to supper and got him drunk, but still Uriah refused to go home to Bathsheba.

Exasperated by Uriah's loyalty, David changed his strategy. He wrote a letter to Uriah's commander Joab that said, "Set Uriah in the forefront of the hardest fighting and then draw back from him, so that he may be struck down and die." (Remember that the next time you hear someone commend the Bible as a wholesome guide to family values.)

What the king ordered was exactly what happened. Uriah was killed, Bathsheba mourned him, and when her mourning was over she became David's wife and bore him a son. But the thing that David had done displeased the Lord and before the baby could make a fist, Nathan the prophet was knocking at the front door of the palace, sent by God to confront the king.

The way he did it was pure genius—not head-on, like a fire and brimstone preacher, but sideways, with a story. Why did he take such an indirect route? Because he had not come to condemn David. That would have been easy enough to do, given the facts at hand, but Nathan was up to something much more profound than that. He had come to change David's life, if he could—to help the king see what he had done so that his conscience was revived and his sense of justice restored. Then Israel might have the king she was supposed to have instead of this handsome hero whose power had begun to stink.

If David could see that—if he could pronounce judgment on himself—the impact would be a hundred times greater than if Nathan did it for him. But it called for real restraint on Nathan's part. He had to contain his anger and resist the temptation to do David's work for him. He had to remember why he had come— not to demolish the king but to bring him back to God—which in this case called for an incredibly light touch.

So Nathan told David a story, knowing good and well how human beings tend to drop their defenses while they are listening to a story about someone else. When words are not aimed right at us, we can listen better. We are freed from our own points of view and can try on all the parts, finding out how different things look through different eyes.

That is what happened to David when Nathan told him about the rich man with many flocks and the poor man with nothing but one little ewe lamb. When the rich man stole the poor man's sheep, David rushed to the poor man's defense and it was not until he had pronounced a death sentence on the rich man that he found out what he had done.

"You are the man!" Nathan told him, and David's heart split in two. "I have sinned against the Lord," he said—not because Nathan had told him so but because he had discovered it for himself, and that was the beginning of his coming back to life again. Technically, it should not have been. He had broken three of the ten commandments in short order—thou shalt not commit adultery, thou shalt not covet, thou shalt not kill. He had confessed his guilt and he had even condemned himself to death, but that was not what God had in mind for him.

"The Lord has put away your sin," Nathan told him. "You shall not die." That was the good news. The bad news was that his child *would* die, because in conceiving him David had utterly scorned the Lord. This may be the hardest part of the story for us—that a child should die for his father's sin—and I neither want nor know how to explain it to you.

There does seem to be an ancient understanding that while God has given us total freedom to decide how we will live, God has also set boundaries on that freedom. So there are moral limits we trespass at our own risk, like those old, old maps that go right to the edge of the known world and then post the warning, "Beyond here lie dragons." We are free to keep going—people do it all the time—but there are consequences, and consequences are different from punishments. I do not believe that God sits just past the boundaries, deciding whether to hit trespassers with a lightning bolt or a sickly child. That would not be freedom. That would just be a booby trap.

Instead, I believe God in all compassion has described for us the way the world works, letting us know that this is not only a material universe we live in but also a moral one, in which ethical acts have consequences just as physical ones do. Drop a stone out a window and it will fall to the ground. Conceive a child, try to pawn it off on another man, then make its mother a widow, and the child will suffer for all of that. Because it is the will of God? I cannot say. All I know is that we live in a web of relationship with God, with one another, and with all creation that responds to the choices we make. When we exercise our freedom in life-giving ways, even the trees clap their hands. And when we exercise it in death-dealing ways, the earth quakes beneath our feet. None of us is morally autonomous. There are realities governing our life together that we cannot go up against without sooner or later discovering the consequences.

When we do discover them—as individuals, as a community, as a nation—God does not turn away from us. God sends us prophets to wake us up, to tell us stories that show us who we really are. If we are lucky enough to feel our hearts split in two, then we may find that even the death sentences we have pronounced upon ourselves are lifted, because the recognition of sin is the beginning of the end of it. The moment we know we are lost and say so out loud, God can hear us to find us and take us home.

Things were never the same for David after "the matter of Uriah the Hittite." He buried his firstborn son. There were lasting consequences to what he had done that he lived with the rest of his life, but the point is that he lived. God took him back, and gave him new opportunities to exercise his God-given freedom. He and Bathsheba had a second son named Solomon, who ruled Israel for forty years with unprecedented wisdom. David's line survived to produce a boy named Jesus, who no doubt heard this same story about his ancestors David and Bathsheba.

Was David a good man or a bad man? You decide. I think he was both, as most of us are. If we remember him as a hero, I hope it is not because of Goliath, or the psalms, or the war stories. I hope it is because of that moment with Nathan, when he saw who he was and said so, so that God could say, "Come home."

Four

I'm Sorry, I Don't Dance

Nebuchadnezzar said to them. "Is it true, O Shadrach, Meshach, and Abednego, that you do not serve my gods and you do not worship the golden statue that I have set up? Now if you are ready when you hear the sound of the horn, pipe, lyre, trigon, harp, drum, and entire musical ensemble to fall down and worship the statue that I have made, well and good. But if you do not worship, you shall immediately be thrown into a furnace of blazing fire, and who is the god that will deliver you out of my hands?"

DANIEL 3:14–15

A COUPLE OF WEEKS AGO I WATCHED A MOVIE CALLED *Clear and Present Danger* with Harrison Ford. If you have seen it, then you know that it is about Jack Ryan, a CIA agent whom the President of the United States assigns to go up against a bunch of Colombian drug lords. Ryan has some idea of doing this legally, but his partner Ritter has a better idea: he sets up a covert military operation behind Ryan's back. By the time Ryan finds out about it, a lot of bombs have exploded and a lot of people have died.

After almost getting killed himself, he winds up in the Oval Office with a nasty looking cut over his right eye, confronting the President about his own part in the scandal. The President denies it at first, but when Ryan announces his intention to take what he knows to the Senate Oversight Committee, the President's face goes slack. Then he begins to grin, and says, "You're not going to do that, Jack. You've got yourself a chip in the big game now. You're going to tuck that away. You're going to save that for a time when your own life is on the line. Then you're going to pull it out and I'm going to cash it in for you."

"I am?" Jack says.

"The country can't afford another deception that goes all the way to the top," the President says. "You'll take the blame, and you will be punished, but it won't amount to much. A slap on the wrist. You know, Jack, the old Potomac two-step."

To which Ryan says, "I'm sorry, Mr. President. I don't dance."

Now that is a great line, but the only reason it worked was that Ryan took no pleasure in saying it. He looked miserable through the whole movie, even at the end when he raised his right hand and swore to tell the truth, the whole truth and nothing but the truth to the Senate. If he had been enjoying himself at that point it would have ruined everything, because then he would have been the object of his own devotion.

Instead, he came across as a servant of the truth, which was more important to him than his own comfort, safety, or reputation. What happened after the credits rolled was anybody's guess. It was entirely possible that Jack Ryan wound up discredited and disgraced by a Senate that supported the President instead of him, but I do not think that would have mattered to Jack. His purpose was not to become a hero. His purpose was to serve the truth.

I give you this extended movie review because I think it will get you in the mood for Daniel. He tells a similar story in his book, about three Jewish princes named Meshach, Shadrach, and Abednego, Persian names given them by King Nebuchadnezzar. Their real names were Hananiah, Mishael, and Azariah—three "young men without physical defect and handsome, versed in every branch of wisdom, endowed with knowledge and insight" (Daniel 1:4).

The king special-ordered them from Jerusalem after he sacked that holy city, along with a bunch of other young nobles whom he meant to train for his court. He brought them to live in the royal palace, taught them Persian literature and language, and fed them from the royal table, or tried to.

Daniel and his three friends stood out from the others because they refused to eat the king's food. Why? Because it was not kosher. Conquered princes from a land that was no more, they remained loyal to their ways. They asked for plain vegetables and water and they got it. Furthermore, they grew fat on it, and when the king examined them after three years of training he found them the brightest and best of the young princes from Israel. He appointed them to his court and relied on their counsel. Eventually he made Daniel governor of Babylon and put Shadrach, Meshach, and Abednego in charge with him.

The kosher food incident should have warned the king that his princes had other loyalties. Some time later, the king erected a huge golden statue in Babylon—nine feet wide and ninety feet high. He invited every VIP in Persia to the dedication ceremony. He hired a huge band to play, and when the day came his herald told all the honored guests what to do. When they heard the band strike up, they were to fall down before the god and worship it. Anyone who failed to do so would be thrown at once into a furnace of blazing fire.

If you have ever taken a pottery class, then you know something about what the furnace looked like. It was a large brick kiln, with one opening at the top and another at ground level—big enough for three or four people to walk around in when it was cold, and big enough to cook the same number when it was hot. Death by fire was a common enough punishment in those days. There were probably as many bones in the furnace as pottery shards, so everyone there that day knew the king meant business.

The furnace was stoked, the band began to play, and everyone who heard it fell on their faces—everyone, that is, except the three Jewish princes way in the back, the same three the king had set above all the rest. They stood there like three tall oaks while everyone else lay face down in the dirt. I expect it humiliated the king, although that was not their purpose. They meant him no disrespect. They simply could not bow down to the statue any-more than they could eat the king's food. They served a higher authority, and however grateful they may have been for the king's favor, their lives did not belong to him. Their lives belonged to God. They would worship no other.

In a furious rage, the king ordered them to the front of the crowd and explained the procedure one last time. When the band played, they were to fall down before the god and worship it. They could do that or they could roast in his own handmade hell. It was their choice. According to Daniel, they answered in unison, "We're sorry, Mr. President. We don't dance."

They were saved, of course. The king was unnerved by the presence of a fourth man inside the furnace—one he did not put there—who looked for all the world like a god. Seeing that mysterious fourth one, he called the whole thing off. Shadrach, Meshach, and Abednego came out of the furnace smelling like roses, not ashes, and the king was so astounded that he promoted them on the spot.

It was the best possible happy ending, which Daniel preserved for all time: obey God and God will rescue you. But I do not think that was the point. According to Shadrach, Meshach, and Abednego, the point was to obey God no matter what. No matter if they died. No matter if anyone ever knew they were right.

When Nebuchadnezzar gave them one last chance to change their minds, they did not presume to tell him what God would do because they did not know. They simply told him what they would not do, in the politest possible terms. "O Nebuchadnezzar, we have no need to present a defense to you in this matter," they said. "If our God whom we serve is able to deliver us from the furnace of blazing fire and out of your hand, O king, let him deliver us. But if not, be it known to you, O king, that we will not serve your gods and we will not worship the golden statue that you have set up" (Daniel 3:16–18).

It was that simple, and as far as I am concerned the high point of the story was right then, when all three of them said, "We will not." Everything that happened after that was extra. The moment of sparkling clarity was the moment when three stubborn human beings declared what—for the love of God—they would not do. Period.

That is what makes this a good story about discipleship, especially the kind that leads to a cross. It shows you how easy it is to get yourself killed, simply by saying, "I'm sorry, I don't dance." To Nebuchadnezzar. To Pilate. To any of the foreign powers who want us to forget who we are and dance to their music. It would be a lot easier for us if we had a real enemy like Nebuchadnezzar to say no to. Instead, most of us face powers that are much more subtly a part of our lives. We have been living in Babylon for so long that it takes special gifts of discernment just to recognize the foreign gods. They do not seem like gods. To us they seem just like the hard realities of modern day life.

One way to discern them is to pay attention to what is going on inside you. When someone in a position of authority asks you to do something that makes you feel queasy, start looking around for a golden statue. When someone asks you to lie about something, or set someone up, and then suggests that there may be dire consequences if you refuse, that ball of fear inside you is a sure sign that you are being recruited to worship a false god. The name of the god does not matter, since it has no life of its own. Its life comes from those who have set it up, and they are always hunting new converts. First they find you, far from home, hungry for something you seem to have lost. They school you in their own literature and language. They offer you rich food and drink from their own tables. They appoint you to positions of power and then one day they invite you to a dedication ceremony, where you are introduced to your new god.

It is very simple, someone tells you. When the band plays, worship the golden statue. Thank him for all your good fortune, and promise him your loyalty from now on. That old god of yours is all worn out, can't you tell? This one is bigger, better, and far more reliable. No more guesswork about where he is or what he is thinking. No more wondering which way to go. With this one, you just bow when someone says bow and good things will keep coming your way. Refuse to bow, and you lose everything.

That is the basic pattern, from before time and forever. Memorize it and you may begin to see it pop up here and there. You may even get your own chance to choose between the golden statue and the furnace. If you do, remember that there are two gods in this story. One is nine feet wide and ninety feet high, located safely outside the furnace. The other is flesh and blood, found inside the furnace—that mysterious fourth one who appears to those who will not dance, walking with them through the midst of the fire.

Five

No Rewards

O Lord, you have enticed me, and I was enticed; you have overpowered me, and you have prevailed. I have become a laughingstock all day long; everyone mocks me. For whenever I speak, I must cry out, I must shout, "Violence and destruction!" For the word of the Lord has become for me a reproach and derision all day long.

JEREMIAH 20:7–8

A WHILE BACK I RECEIVED A LONG LETTER FROM someone who is struggling with his faith. He has been God-haunted for years now, but he is also a husband and father of two small children. His sense of responsibility to his family keeps his wilder impulses in check. Sometimes I think that if he were not expected at home to help bathe the kids and put them to bed, he would be gone—off to search the world for food for his starving heart.

Meanwhile, he works in the personnel department of a large plant, where his advocacy of employees keeps getting him in trouble with management. His office has been moved twice, further and further away from the corridor of power where decisions are made. Pretty soon, he says, they will build him a little shed out in the yard with a tin-can telephone.

The letter he wrote me is about his frustration with the

Christian faith—not only his disappointment with the institutional church, but also his distrust of the gospel. "How do I know that if I invest the effort and risk whatever shred of dignity I have left it will work for me? If I witness and evangelize, if I quit drinking and throwing money away, if I pray every night, read the Bible daily, take my family to church every Sunday, if I speak out at work against racism, sexism, exploitation of any kind, will I be a man transformed or just unemployed, known only for his foolish hypocrisy?"

I think of him when I read the book of the prophet Jeremiah, because the two of them have similar complaints with God. Jeremiah's is considerably louder—he was one of the major prophets, after all, who foresaw the destruction of Judah—but his lament is universal in its anguish: "O Lord, you have enticed me, and I was enticed; you have overpowered me, and you have prevailed."

The flavor of the original Hebrew is richer than we have in our English translation: "O Lord, you have seduced me, and I was seduced: you have forced your will on me and you have won." It is strong language, essentially accusing God of spiritual rape, and most scholars are skittish about it, calling the lament "almost blasphemy." They explain that Jeremiah was near the breaking point, having just spent the night in stocks after a public beating by Pashur the high priest and chief of police.

Was that any place for God's anointed prophet? Bound hand and foot like a common pickpocket, with a black eye and a bloody nose to announce to anyone who saw him that he had lost the fight? It was not right. None of it was his idea. He was doing exactly what God had asked him to do, saying exactly what God had told him to say, and absolutely nothing was happening. Or nothing constructive, anyway. He had become a local joke. Beggars looked down on him. Children mocked him while their parents chuckled. Even his friends had deserted him, put off by his endless tirades.

"Violence and destruction!" That was the message God had given him to proclaim, although there was no evidence that the message was true. Everything seemed fine to the people of Judah. They were prosperous. Their national defense was strong. They had worked out a comfortable relationship with God, whom they did not bother unless they needed something. Jeremiah was the person God had sent to wake them up, but no one was listening. And Jeremiah, for his part, was bitterly disappointed that the same God who sent him could not arrange a better reception for him. "O Lord, you have seduced me, and I was seduced."

His complaint raises the question of his expectations. What did Jeremiah think God had promised him that he did not get? What was it that he found so enticing? The seduction language is intriguing at this point, because the most powerful seducer in the world still needs someone who is vulnerable to being seduced— someone who is so hungry, or so dreamy, or so innocent that he ignores all the warning signals, seeing only what he wants to see. The seducer dangles something shiny in front of him and he bites, but the hook is always hidden inside something he is genuinely hungry for.

What is the best bait? When it is spiritual seduction you are talking about, the possibilities are vast. I suppose one enticement that works on most believers is the lure of effectiveness. If you could have asked Jeremiah what he wanted, I bet he would have told you that all he wanted was for people to listen to him—that he did not care what they did to him as long as they took his message to heart. It is the wish to be effective, and I do not know anyone who is immune to it, but neither do I know many people who will stop at that.

It usually leads to the wish to be respected and obeyed, because who is going to listen to you, after all, unless they hold you in some esteem? This bait is especially attractive to clergy. When we say, "Let us pray," we expect people to bow their heads, and God help the person who interrupts one of our sermons. ("Would one of the ushers please show this gentleman out?") What wouldn't Jeremiah have given for one moment of power like that? Instead, he was the one who was always being shown the way out, and not like a gentleman.

The most common enticement I can think of, though, is the lure of reward—that those who are faithful to God will be protected, rescued, defended, upheld. You hear it all the time. "She is such a wonderful woman. I can't believe how people take advantage of her." Or, "Why did that happen to him, of all people? He is the most faithful man I know." We have a strange, built-in sense that those who love God will find their way strewn with flowers, that people will stand back when we pass by and say, "My, aren't you something?"

A friend of mine still remembers the year he and a lawyer friend decided to prepare Christmas baskets for the elderly residents of a housing project high rise. They bought canned hams, sweet potatoes, and fresh Florida oranges, hard candies wrapped like Christmas ornaments and chocolate bars shaped like Santa Claus. They arranged all of this beautifully in two dozen baskets, loaded them all in the lawyer's car and set off for downtown Atlanta.

At the high rise, they took over one of the four elevators and started working their way to the top, floor by floor. The first couple of stops went fine. One of them held the elevator doors open while the other one delivered the baskets. Then on about the fourth floor a gnarled old man stepped into the elevator and pressed the button for the fifteenth floor.

Santa's helpers looked at each other over their baskets with palpable alarm. "Sir," one of them said, with great sensitivity, "we are using this elevator to deliver these Christmas baskets. Would you mind using one of the others?"

"This here is my elevator," the old man muttered. The other two laughed amicably. "I see," one of them said. "Well just for today, could you use one of the others so that we can deliver these baskets?"

"I told you this is my elevator," the old man said. "You boys go get yourselves one of the others." And he turned into im-movable stone on the spot. So my friend and his friend un-loaded everything into the hallway and stood there quivering with righteous indignation as the doors closed on the old man and took him away.

"We were doing God's work!" my friend says, remembering his outrage. "We didn't have to be there on Christmas Eve, riding a smelly elevator in that godawful place. We put ourselves at risk! Why, we even left a Mercedes convertible parked on the street!"

He finds the memory pretty funny now. A little further into his discipleship, he now knows that no good deed goes unpunished, but he still longs to be appreciated. He is still enticed by the idea that doing God's work will make him glow in the dark so that everyone knows how special he is. It is a seductive idea, and he is not the only one who has fallen for it, is he? Still, it is a fiction, a figment of our own imaginations.

What the Bible tells us over and over again—what our lives tell us—is that the only reward for doing God's work is doing God's work. Period. Furthermore, if we do it really well, we are likely to get ourselves killed. Or at least sent to the doghouse, whether that is a shed in the yard with a tin-can telephone or a night in stocks after a run-in with the chief of police. That is what success looks like in the upside-down kingdom of God, and so far as I know no one has ever liked it.

Do you know Saint Teresa of Avila? Back in the sixteenth

century, after a particularly difficult day, she shook her fist at God. "It's no wonder you have so few friends," she shouted, "if this is how you treat them!"

On Palm Sunday, you can walk into just about any church in the land and hear the story of what happened to God's *best* friend, whose reward for perfect obedience was death on a cross. And yet we line up to worship him, which is a very puzzling thing. How—with a Lord like that—did we ever get the idea that our faith should win us respect, or influence, or protection? When did he ever tell us that the gospel would "work"?

Either we have been seduced, or else we have glimpsed something in him that eclipses all our self-seeking fantasies. I would try to describe it, but it would just end up sounding like all the other rewards we look for. There was no reward. There is no reward. There is only the self-annihilating love of God, who raises us from the dead.

✤ God's Daring Plan

Six

God's Daring Plan

In that region there were shepherds living in the fields, keeping watch over their flock by night. Then an angel of the Lord stood before them, and the glory of the Lord shone around them, and they were terrified.

LUKE 2:8–9

ONCE UPON A TIME—OR BEFORE TIME, ACTUALLY, before there were clocks or calendars or Christmas trees— God was all there was. No one knows anything about that time because no one was there to know it, but somewhere in the middle of that time before time, God decided to make a world. Maybe God was bored or maybe God was lonely or maybe God just liked to make things and thought it was time to try something big.

Whatever the reason, God made a world—this world—and filled it with the most astonishing things: with humpback whales that sing and white-striped skunks that stink and birds with more colors on them than a box of Crayola crayons. The list is way too long to go into here, but suffice it to say that at the end when God stood back and looked at it all, God was pleased. Only something was missing. God could not think what it was at first, but slowly it dawned on him.

Everything he had made was interesting and gorgeous and it

all fit together really well, only there was nothing in the world that looked like him, exactly. It was as if he had painted this huge masterpiece and then forgotten to sign it, so he got busy making his signature piece, something made in his own image, so that anyone who looked at it would know who the artist was.

He had one single thing in mind at first, but as he worked God realized that one thing all by itself was not the kind of statement he wanted to make. He knew what it was like to be alone, and now that he had made a world he knew what it was like to have company, and company was definitely better. So God decided to make two things instead of one, which were alike but different, and both would be reflections of him—a man and a woman who could keep him and each other company.

Flesh was what he made them out of—flesh and blood—a wonderful medium, extremely flexible and warm to the touch. Since God, strictly speaking, was not made out of anything at all, but was pure mind, pure spirit, he was very taken with flesh and blood. Watching his two creatures stretch and yawn, laugh and run, he found to his surprise that he was more than a little envious of them. He had made them, it was true, and he knew how fragile they were, but their very breakability made them more touching to him, somehow. It was not long before God found himself falling in love with them. He liked being with them better than any of the other creatures he had made, and he especially liked walking with them in the garden in the cool of the evening.

It almost broke God's heart when they got together behind his back, did the one thing he had asked them not to do and then hid from him—from *him!*—while he searched the garden until way past dark, calling their names over and over again. Things were different after that. God still loved the human creatures best of all, but the attraction was not mutual. Birds were crazy about God, especially ruby-throated hummingbirds. Dolphins and raccoons could not get enough of him, but human beings had other things on their minds. They were busy learning how to make things, grow things, buy things, sell things, and the more they learned to do for themselves, the less they depended on God. Night after night he threw pebbles at their windows, inviting them to go for a walk with him, but they said they were sorry, they were busy.

It was not long before most human beings forgot all about him. They called themselves "self-made" men and women, as if that were a plus and not a minus. They honestly believed they had created themselves, and they liked the result so much that they divided themselves into groups of people who looked, thought, and talked alike. Those who still believed in God drew pictures of him that looked just like them, and that made it easier for them to turn away from the people who were different. You would not believe the trouble this got them into: everything from armed warfare to cities split right down the middle, with one kind of people living on that side of the line and another kind on the other.

God would have put a stop to it all right there, except for one thing. When he had made human beings, he had made them free. That was built into them just like their hearts and brains were, and even God could not take it back without killing them. So God left them free, and it almost killed *him* to see what they were doing to each other.

God shouted to them from the sidelines, using every means he could think of, including floods, famines, messengers, and manna. He got inside people's dreams, and if that did not work he woke them up in the middle of the night with his whispering. No matter what he tried, however, he came up against the barriers of flesh and blood. They were made of it and he was not, which made translation difficult. God would say, "Please stop before you destroy yourselves!" but all they could hear was thunder. God would say, "I love you as much now as the day I made you," but all they could hear was a loon calling across the water.

Babies were the exception to this sad state of affairs. While their parents were all but deaf to God's messages, babies did not have any trouble hearing him at all. They were all the time laughing at God's jokes or crying with him when he cried, which went right over their parents' heads. "Colic," the grown-ups would say, or "Isn't she cute? She's laughing at the dust mites in the sunlight." Only she wasn't, of course. She was laughing because God had just told her it was cleaning day in heaven, and that what she saw were fallen stars the angels were shaking from their feather dusters.

Babies did not go to war. They never made hate speeches or littered or refused to play with each other because they belonged to different political parties. They depended on other people for everything necessary to their lives and a phrase like "self-made babies" would have made them laugh until their bellies hurt. While no one asked their opinions about anything that mattered (which would have been a smart thing to do), almost everyone seemed to love them, and that gave God an idea.

Why not create himself as one of these delightful creatures?

He tried the idea out on his cabinet of archangels and at first they were all very quiet. Finally the senior archangel stepped forward to speak for all of them. He told God how much they would worry about him, if he did that. He would be putting himself at the mercy of his creatures, the angel said. People could do anything they wanted to him, and if he seriously meant to become one of them there would be no escape for him if things turned sour. Could he at least create himself as a magical baby with special powers? It would not take much—just the power to become invisible, maybe, or the power to hurl bolts of lightning if the need arose. The baby idea was a stroke of genius, the angel said, it really was, but it lacked adequate safety features.

God thanked the archangels for their concern but said no, he thought he would just be a regular baby. How else could he gain the trust of his creatures? How else could he persuade them that he knew their lives inside out, unless he lived one like theirs? There was a risk. He knew that. Okay, there was a *high* risk, but that was part of what he wanted his creatures to know: that he was willing to risk everything to get close to them, in hopes that they might love him again.

It was a daring plan, but once the angels saw that God was dead set on it, they broke into applause—not the uproarious kind but the steady kind that goes on and on when you have witnessed something you know you will never see again.

While they were still clapping, God turned around and left the cabinet chamber, shedding his robes as he went. The angels watched as his midnight blue mantle fell to the floor, so that all the stars on it collapsed in a heap. Then a strange thing happened. Where the robes had fallen, the floor melted and opened up to reveal a scrubby brown pasture speckled with sheep and—right in the middle of them—a bunch of shepherds sitting around a camp-fire drinking wine out of a skin. It was hard to say who was more startled, the shepherds or the angels, but as the shepherds looked up at them, the angels pushed their senior member to the edge of the hole. Looking down at the human beings who were all trying to hide behind each other (poor things, no wings), the angel said in as gentle a voice as he could muster, "Do not be afraid; for see—I am bringing you good news of great joy for all the people: to you is born this day in the city of David a savior, who is the Messiah, the Lord."

And away up the hill, from the direction of town, came the sound of a newborn baby's cry.

Seven

The Wilderness Exam

*Then Jesus was led up by the Spirit into the wilderness to be
tempted by the devil. He fasted forty days and forty nights, and
afterwards he was famished.*

MATTHEW 4:1–2

THE SEASON OF LENT ALWAYS BEGINS WITH JESUS
sitting in the wilderness, being tempted by the devil. His
hair is still wet from his baptism by John. No sooner did he come
out of the water than the dove that had lit on him turned into a
guide bird, leading him away from the river and into the desert
with the voice of God still ringing in his ears: "This is my Son,
the Beloved, with whom I am well pleased."

What remained to be seen was what that meant, exactly. How
would God's Beloved behave? What would he say, do, stand for,
oppose? Would God give him special powers or would he make do
with the standard human equipment package? No one knew any
of that yet, perhaps not even Jesus. He had been ordained by God
at the river, but his ministry had not yet begun. There were some
things to be settled first, some tests to be passed. Interestingly
enough, God did not administer them but let the devil do it, which
points to a strange kind of partnership here. Jesus did not wander
into the wilderness by mistake, after all. He was led there by the
Spirit, who delivered him to the devil for his forty day exam.

Actually, the exam came at the *end* of those forty days, when Jesus was famished. His examiner knew better than to start when he was fresh and well fed. He let Jesus stew first, watching from a distance as God's Beloved said his prayers. The first couple of weeks he said them standing up. Then when his legs gave out he said them sitting down and finally, near the end, he said them lying flat on the ground with his belt cinched up as tight as it would go. That was when the devil knew it was time to start, when Jesus had run out of his own resources and might be open to accepting a little help.

I sat in the desert once myself, just to see what it was like. The first thing I noticed was how quiet it was, so quiet that I could hear the racket my body makes—gurgle, wheeze, thump. Did you know that if you can get quiet enough, you can actually hear the hum of your own electricity? It makes about as much noise as the motor on a small electric clock, only most of us cannot hear it because of all the other motors around us. In the desert, you can.

The second thing I noticed was how fast I got lonely. There is something about a desert that can suck all the self-confidence right out of you. It is so big, so quiet, so empty that you cannot help noticing how small and perishable you are. You remember that you are dust and to dust you shall return. You wish you had someone to distract you from that fact, or at least someone to talk to about it. Anyone but the devil, that is.

The third thing I noticed was the flies. Matthew never mentions the flies, but based on my own experience I feel certain that if they did not constitute a fourth temptation for Jesus then they at least made the other three harder for him to bear, because nothing can try your spirit like a fly. There I was in the desert, trying to commune with Jesus, and all I could think about was that #*@! fly—circling my head, buzzing in my ears, trying to crawl up my nose. Flies are perfect tools of the devil: "So you think you're pretty spiritual, huh? Well, try one of these on for size."

On a scale of one to a hundred, my desert experience was about a .25 compared to Jesus', but I tell you about it in order to remind you of your own quiet, lonely, vulnerable times. Have you ever been hungry like that? Have you ever felt the devil nipping at your heels? If you have, then you know something about the desert, and I bet one of the things you know is how much you can wonder where God is when you have been stranded there for a while. Why doesn't God send a rescue team, or at least a raven with some bread? Why doesn't God give you the power to rear up and roar so loud at the devil that he runs away and never comes back?

I cannot help thinking that something like that was going on with Jesus in the wilderness. Remember that he had just come from his own baptism, where everyone present had seen the sky break open, watched the dove descend and heard the voice from heaven introduce God's own son. After something like that, everyone, including Jesus, might have expected him to sprout wings and fly away. They might have looked for him to become a kind of super hero, who would cease being human in order to rescue human beings, showing up in the nick of time to snatch them out of danger.

Only that was not what happened. What happened was that he went from one spectacular moment to a long, lonely time in the wilderness, during which he may have wondered if he had imagined the whole thing. For forty days and forty nights there was no sign of God at all. The sky stayed shut. There were no doves. No voice from heaven spoke reassuring words. There was just him, the desert, and finally, the devil.

You already know their conversation by heart, so I will not go over it again. The important thing to notice is what was on the devil's test. First he tempted Jesus to practice magic: *Command these stones to become loaves of bread.* Next he tempted Jesus to call on God for special protection: *Throw yourself down from the temple.* Finally he tempted him to take control of all the kingdoms of the world: *All these I will give you, if you will fall down and worship me.*

All along, the devil subtly suggested that Jesus deserved better than God was giving him. Why should the son of God be famished? Why should he so much as stub his toe, or be subject to Caesar when Caesar should be subject to him? If God could not do better than that by his son, the devil suggested, maybe Jesus should start shopping around for another father.

Listen to how the devil begins two of his three tests: "If you are the son of God. . . ." He is daring Jesus to prove who he is by acting like a god instead of a man, and if Jesus is not really tempted by that idea then this is not really a test.

It is only a test if he is *sorely* tempted—to rise above the hunger, the danger, the helplessness of the human condition and seize something better for himself—to make himself a hot bun breakfast, after all that time; to whistle up some angel bodyguards and start planning his inauguration as president of the world. He is the son of God, after all.

This is the story in which everyone finds out what being the son of God really means. This is the story in which Jesus proves who he is not by seizing power, but by turning it down. God's Beloved will not practice magic. He will not ask for special protection or seek political power. As much as it may surprise everyone, including him, he will remain human, accepting all the usual risks.

It is, after all, the only way humans will ever learn what "son of God" really means. A son of God is not someone who is related to God by rising out of his humanity, but someone who is beloved by God for sinking into it even when he is famished, even when he is taunted by the devil himself. It is someone who can listen to every good reason in the world for becoming God's rival and remain God's child instead.

This is chiefly a story about Jesus' identity, but insofar as we belong to him, it is a story about our identity, too. There are plenty of times when we too are tempted to believe that we deserve bigger and better than what we have. That devilish voice in our heads says things like, "If you are a child of God, shouldn't things be going a little smoother for you? If you are really a Christian, I mean—shouldn't you be happier, healthier, richer, safer?"

You know what to say back now, right? "Away with you, Satan! I would rather be a hungry child of God than a well-fed player on your team. Now shoo!"

If you can manage that, then chances are very good that you will hear another voice in your head before long, ten thousand times more beautiful than the first. "This is my beloved child," the voice will say, "in whom I am well pleased."

Eight

The Trickle-Up Effect

James and John, the sons of Zebedee, came forward to him and said to him, "Teacher, we want you to do for us whatever we ask of you." And he said to them, "What is it you want me to do for you?" And they said to him, "Grant us to sit, one at your right hand and one at your left, in your glory."

MARK 10:35–37

O N THE WHOLE I AM PRETTY IGNORANT ABOUT CUR-
rent events, but recently I spent nine hours on an airplane where there was nothing to do but read, sleep, and play cards. I was not sleepy and I did not have a deck of cards, so I read most of the time. First my book, which only lasted about three hours, and then six news magazines in a row. It was like a crash course in American culture, where most of the same stories came up over and over again: Haiti, health care, Bosnia, Israel.

One word central to all of them was the word "power." It was used over and over again, in differing contexts, until I began to wonder. What is power, exactly? How does it work and who has it? In the world of news magazine headlines, power is the ability to influence or control other people's lives. It may be political power like Bill Clinton's, or financial power like Donald Trump's. It may be spiritual power like Pope Paul's or star power like Barbra Streisand's.

Whatever kind it is, power thrives in the rare air at the top of any given hierarchy, where those who have it generally require tinted windows and bodyguards. One sure sign that people have power is that other people want to get near them—to photograph them, to attack them, to cheer them, to inhale them—it hardly matters what their motives are. It is the power itself they cannot resist, the chance to get close to someone who has something they do not in hopes that some of it will rub off on them. This fascination with power has been going on forever. It is how the world works. Those who have it get to make the rules and write history, but they have to keep an eye out because power is slippery and those who do not have it are always ready to yank it out from under those who do. There are only so many head tables in the world, after all, and the game of musical chairs never stops.

Every now and then the powerless become powerful and nine times out of ten they turn out to be as heartless as their predecessors. And yet most of us have this abiding hope that if only the right people can get into power and stay there, without letting their power corrupt them, then the world will be a better place. That is why we campaign for people. That is why we vote for them. Because we want them to sit at the head table and make good decisions for us.

If you ask me, the Zebedee brothers are thinking of election day in the tenth chapter of Mark's gospel. Not election day for Galilee County but God's election day, when their very own teacher Jesus would come into his own. He has just told them what that will mean for him—sure suffering and certain death—but it simply does not register. They are focused on his power, which has been evident from the very first day they met him. They could sense it even when he was not doing anything fancy—he had this gravity about him, this electricity. He had power, and whatever else might happen to him along the way, they knew he was headed straight to the top—to glory—and as far as they were concerned there was no one better for the job.

You can hardly blame them for wanting to go with him. "Teacher," they say to him, "we want you to do for us whatever we ask of you." What they want, it turns out, are top-ranking cabinet appointments. When the kingdom comes, they want to sit as close to Jesus as they can, and while this may be an example of gross ambition on their part, it may also be a case of profound faith. James and John absolutely believe that Jesus will reign. In spite of his dire predictions, in spite of the storm clouds gathering on the horizon ahead of them, they are so sure of Jesus' final victory that they sign up to go with him.

This is not unreasonable, since they have been his chief assistants from the start. Along with Peter, they are Jesus' closest friends, the ones he takes with him when he leaves the others at home. So it is natural for them to want to stay near him and they seem willing to do whatever it takes. "Are you able to drink the cup that I drink," he asks them, "or be baptized with the baptism that I am baptized with?" Although they do not know what they are saying, they do not hesitate. "We are able," they say in unison, and then Jesus tries one more time to tell them how things are.

They seem to believe that the new world will be set up just like the old world only with new leadership in place. The bad guys at the head table will be removed, their chairs will be fumigated and God's new crew will be seated, with Jesus in the number one position and the most loyal members of his campaign staff on either side of him. Once this change has been accomplished, then—finally! at last!—the good people will commence to redeem the world from top to bottom, beginning from the top. The ultimate trickle-down effect.

"It doesn't work that way," Jesus tells them one more time. The new world is not remotely like the old one. It turns the old one upside down. The number ones are not the powerful ones having their pictures taken at the head of the table; they are the quiet ones slipping in and out among the guests, refilling wine glasses and laying down clean silverware for the next course. The great ones are not the dignitaries to the left and right of the ruler; they are the slaves who are stirring pots in the kitchen, testing the temperature of the soup so that it is neither too hot nor too cold for the honored guests. James and John want Jesus to hurry up and become king of the world, but he has other things on his mind. Has everyone been served? Is all the food on the table? Does anyone need anything? "For the Son of Man came not to be served but to serve, and to give his life as a ransom for many."

We have heard this teaching so many times that it is all but lost on us. The end of the line is the best place to be. The lowliest job is the one to covet. Those who serve are luckier than those in power, and lovers of God get less status, not more. It is incomprehensible in terms of the world we live in. Things simply do not work that way. The only way to make any sense out of it at all is to think of it as some sort of intermediate stage, like boot camp or parole. Do your time as a servant with no whining and win two good seats in the kingdom to come.

"It doesn't work that way," Jesus tells them one more time. He is not pretending to be a servant until the time comes for him to whip off his disguise and climb onto his throne; he is a servant through and through. The good seats are not his to give. He does not even have one himself. Someone else is in charge of all that, someone he is too shy even to name, whom it is his sole pleasure and purpose to serve.

He is not in it for reward. He is in it for the love of God, which promises him nothing but the opportunity to give himself away. The best seat he will get this side of the grave is a throne full of splinters, and when he is hung out on it to dry by the powers that be, it will not be James and John on either side of him but two unnamed bandits, one on his left and the other on his right.

If we do not understand it, we should not be too hard on ourselves. No one ever has, not really—not Peter, not James, not John, nor any of the others who were nearest and dearest to him. If we understand any better than they did, it is only because Jesus is still serving us, still feeding us, still giving himself away for us. That is the only example of power he will give us, so maybe the best we can do is to grab hold of the mystery any way we can and hang on for dear life.

This much is for sure: whether we can make sense of it or not, serving is how we will transform the world, not from the top down but from the bottom up. The ultimate trickle-up effect. Our leaders can be servants, and the best ones will be, but we must never surrender our power to the powerful. The power God has given us is the strongest stuff in the world: the power to serve, which is the power to turn the Zebedee brothers' question upside down. "Teacher, we want to do for you whatever you ask of us."

Nine

High-Priced Discipleship

⟶

Whoever comes to me and does not hate father and mother,
wife and children, brothers and sisters, yes, and even life itself,
cannot be my disciple.

LUKE 14:26

A FTER CAREFUL CONSIDERATION OF JESUS' HARDER
sayings, I have to conclude that he would not have made a
good parish minister. So much of the job depends on making it
easy for people to come to church and rewarding for them to stay.
Talk to any of the church growth experts and they will tell you
how important it is to create a safe, caring environment where
people believe their concerns will be heard and their needs will
be met. The basic idea is to find out what people are looking for
and to give it to them, so that they decide to stay put instead of
continuing to shop for a church down the street.

This effort to please does not stop once people decide to join
the church. A good parish minister will work hard to make sure
that worship is satisfying, that Christian education is appealing,
that plenty of opportunities for fellowship and service exist. A
well-run church is like a well-run home, where members can
count on regular meals in pleasant surroundings, with people who
generally mind their manners. It matches the American ideal of
Christians as upstanding and good-hearted citizens. When I hear

people talk about Christian virtues and values, it is hard to imagine anyone but Norman Rockwell doing the illustrations: a third-grade classroom full of little girls with blond pigtails and little boys with slingshots in their back pockets, all of them bowing their heads in prayer; families gathered around a Thanksgiving dinner table, with a carving knife in father's hand and a slotted spoon in mother's, while all the children wait eagerly to be served; a bench at the general store, where the milkman, the mailman, and the newspaper boy all stop to share a dozen doughnuts before getting on with the day's work.

There is nothing intrinsically wrong with these pictures, but according to Jesus we cannot be his disciples unless we hate our families, carry our crosses, and give up all our possessions. So why don't we all—preachers and believers alike—just turn in our resignations right now? Because clearly, none of us has what it takes. If Jesus were in charge of an average congregation I figure there would be about four people left there on Sunday mornings, and chances are those four would be fooling themselves. Jesus would greet newcomers by saying, "Are you absolutely sure you want to follow this way of life? It will take everything you have. It has to come before everything else that matters to you. Plenty of people have launched out on it without counting the cost, and as you can see they are not here anymore. The other thing is, if you succeed—if you really do follow me—it will probably get you killed. Why don't you go home and think it over? I would hate for you to get in over your head."

He is the complete opposite of the good parish minister. Far from trying to make it easier for people to follow him, he points out how hard it is. Look at the fourteenth chapter of Luke, where Jesus is talking to a large crowd that has begun trailing him from town to town. They are not people whom he has called to follow him. They have simply shown up, bubbling with enthusiasm, but

Jesus is less than welcoming. He tells them not to get their hopes up, that more than likely they cannot afford what they want. He suggests that they go home and do some sober feasibility studies before they decide to go with him, and I expect that some of them are puzzled by his response.

They all want to go with him. They want to get as close as they can to the energy that radiates from him like heat from a coal. They want to be the first to hear what he says next—to be part of changing the world with him—and they do not have a clue what it costs. Jesus wants to tell them, because the worst thing he can do is to mislead them and let them believe they are running off with the circus when they are in fact headed into battle unarmed.

Why does he say all these disturbing things about hating their parents, their children, their lives? One possibility is that he was using a figure of speech we do not use anymore. In his day, the way you stated a preference was by pairing two things and saying you loved one and hated the other. It did not have anything to do with emotions. It was a matter of priorities, so if I said, "I love the mountains and hate the beach," it would not actually mean I felt hostile toward the ocean, but simply mean that the mountains were my first choice.

I know that does not help much, but it seems worth mentioning since priorities are on Jesus' mind in this passage. He is on his way to Jerusalem, and he knows what a hard road he has ahead of him. Luke knows even more. When he wrote his gospel, Christians were already being persecuted for following Jesus. To have a Christian in the family was dangerous for everyone, because the Romans were thorough. If they found one believer in a household they would arrest everyone, so it really was true that turning toward Jesus meant turning away from your family, whether you wanted to or not. Once you made following Jesus your first priority, everything else fell by the wayside—not because God took it away from you but because that is how the world works. As long as the world opposes those who set out to transform it, the transformers will pay a high price. Ask Harry Wu, Nelson Mandela, and Aung San Suu Kyi. No one tangles with the powers that be and gets away unscathed.

I think that is what Jesus wants us to know. He is not threatening us. He is loving us, as usual—refusing to lie to us, refusing to make his way sound easier than it is. He wants us to know very clearly what it costs so that no one follows him under false pretenses. He does not want us to get halfway through building a tower and have to abandon it, or to go charging into battle without the troops we need to prevail. If all that sounds overly dramatic, then maybe we have lost track of what following him is all about.

Is it about being good, stable citizens or is it about changing the world? Is it about creating a safe, caring environment where people's needs will be met or is it about living such a different way of life that those in authority get mad enough to kill us? Ernie Campbell, one of the great old-time preachers, once said, "If I'm following Jesus, why am I such a good insurance risk?"

"Whoever comes to me and does not hate father and mother, wife and children, brothers and sisters, yes, and even life itself, cannot be my disciple." Discipleship costs all that we have, all that we love, all that we are. That is less God's doing than our own. If the world were kinder to its reformers, discipleship might be a piece of cake, but it is not, and Jesus does not want anyone to be fooled.

He may not have made a good parish minister, but he made a very good savior, and I do not think he is through saving us yet. His best tool has always been the very thing that killed him— that cross he ended up on—the one he was carrying long before he got to Golgotha. He is always offering to share it with us, to let us get underneath it with him. Not, I think, because he wants us to suffer but because he wants us to know how alive you can feel even underneath something that heavy and how it can take your breath away to get hold of your one true necessity. Even suffering itself pales next to what God is doing through it, through you, because you are willing to put yourself in the way.

It is not for everyone. That is clearly what he is telling us. There are not a lot of people who have what it takes to shoulder the cross, but I do not think that means the rest of us are lost. It is for the rest of us—the weak ones—that he took its weight upon himself. If we cannot help him carry it, he will carry us too. I think he just wants us not to take it for granted. I think he just wants us to know what it costs.

Ten

The Hidden I Am

—

The Jews said to him, "Now we know that you have a demon. Abraham died, and so did the prophets; yet you say, "Whoever keeps my word will never taste death.' Are you greater than our father Abraham, who died? The prophets also died. Who do you claim to be?"

JOHN 8:52–53

Y OU NEVER HEAR THE EIGHTH CHAPTER OF JOHN read in church on a Sunday. I am not sure why that is. Maybe it is the bad language: Jesus and the Pharisees, slugging it out, proving that holy men can insult each other as brilliantly as anyone. Jesus tells them they are illegitimate, lying children, born of the devil, who will die in their sins. They tell him he is a suicidal Samaritan possessed by a demon.

"Who do you claim to be?" they ask him at last, getting down to the heart of the matter. Is he a blasphemer or just a kook? But he does not answer them, or he cannot answer them, because it is impossible for him to reveal himself. Only God can do that, he says, and it is not time yet. But he knows God—he is very clear about that—and he keeps God's word.

So far, so good. But then he suggests that he also knows Abraham, who died a couple of thousand years before Jesus was ever born, and that Abraham was happy to look into the future and see Jesus come into his own. This definitely increases his kook potential, but it also raises a graver suspicion. Who *does* Jesus claim to be? Is he suggesting that he operates outside time and space, that he inhabits the reaches of eternity? Only one being does that. Who does this guy think he is? Jesus does not leave them in suspense for long. "Before Abraham was, I am," he says, and they reach down to pick up rocks.

It is not the business about Abraham that sets them off. It is that name again, that name he insists on using for himself that *no one* uses, that no one even says out loud because it is so holy. "I am," he says, and he is not just mixing his verb tenses. He knows what he is doing. He knows what he is saying.

"I am who I am," God announced to Moses from the burning bush. "I am," Jesus echoes (which is to say, "Yahweh") and how dare he? That is what his opponents want to know. How dare he trespass on that name as if it had anything to do with him, as if he had any claim on it at all? "Before Abraham was, I am," he says, and they pick up rocks to throw at him—not to scare him, or to bruise him, but to put him to death.

It is one of those episodes that reminds me how few choices we have when it comes down to deciding who Jesus really is. In his book *The Case for Christianity*, C. S. Lewis declares that a man who said the sort of things Jesus said would not be considered a great moral teacher. He would either be a lunatic—on the same level with a man who claimed to be a poached egg—or else he would be of the devil. "You must make your choice," Lewis says. "Either this man was, and is, the Son of God: or else a madman or something worse. You can shut him up for a fool; you can spit at Him and kill Him as a demon, or you can fall at His feet and call him Lord and God. But don't let us come with any patronizing nonsense about His being a great human teacher. He hasn't left that open to us. He didn't intend to."[1]

When you look at it like that, it is not hard to have some sympathy for the first human beings who had to decide who he was, especially since they had so little to go on. Think about it. They had no resurrection stories to refer to, no New Testament to read. They had no Christmas carols and Easter parades to fall back on. All they had were some prophecies that could be read a dozen different ways, and a first commandment that was written on their hearts in capital letters: "YOU SHALL HAVE NO OTHER GODS BEFORE ME."

That was what they had been taught all their lives. That was the law laid down for them by the one God, who claimed to be a jealous God and who was not above proving it. Then along comes a man who challenges all of that, daring them to believe that he too is God, of one being with the Father who has sent him.

There are those of us who like to think that we could walk right into any room and pick him out, and that there is something wrong with anyone who could not, but I wonder. All we really have going for us is hindsight. We know who Jesus turned out to be. We grew up singing "Jesus loves me, this I know . . ." but what if we did *not* know? What if a very strange man were to stand up in church and say, "You are so far off track you don't even know it. My name is Yahweh. I have come from before time to remind you who you are. I have come from heaven to show you the way home." When he turned around and walked out the door, how many of us would follow?

It is not a fair question, because we cannot give back what we already know, but this hindsight business is true. You know how true it is in daily life. You can never see the shape of the mountain while you are heaving yourself over it. It is only afterwards, looking at it from a crackling fire down in the valley, that you can see where you have been. Jesus knew that the same thing was true about the religious life as well.

"When you have lifted up the Son of Man, then you will know that I am," he said a little earlier. After you have strung me up, after you have watched me die, after you have come looking for my body and cannot find it anywhere, then you will know who I am. You will recognize me when I am gone.

Many years ago now, when I was in seminary, I stayed on campus over one particular spring break. Since the refectory was closed, I stocked my refrigerator with cold cuts and vegetables and spent my days in the library reading. I had the place to myself, and while it was a luxury it was also a little eerie to walk down the halls with nothing but the sound of my own feet patting the linoleum behind me.

One afternoon I needed a break from my books and walked down to what we called the Red Table Cafe—a room full of vending machines in the basement under the chapel, with one round table and four wooden chairs painted fire-engine red. I did not expect anyone to be there, so I was startled to find a man sitting in one of the chairs nursing a paper cup full of coffee.

I knew right away that he was not a student, although he may have been, once. When he looked up at me his face was wide open and interesting. He had the bluest possible eyes and there was definitely someone home in them, but he seemed to have fallen on hard times. His windbreaker was greasy around the cuffs. The collar of his flannel shirt was frayed. The fingers he curled around his cup were dirty and they held on a little too tight.

"Hello," he said. It was a nice voice, soft but direct.

"Hello," I said, wondering if it was wise to start a conversation with him. But he wanted to talk, and before long I learned that he had been on the road for a while, hitchhiking from somewhere to somewhere else, and that when his latest ride had let him off about a mile away he had decided to walk up to the divinity school and take a look around.

"I was here a long, long time ago," he said, smiling into his coffee cup.

"A student?" I asked. I was shocked. What had happened to him?

"No," he said, "a speaker. But like I said, that was a long time ago." We both looked at his cup until he changed the subject. "Is the refectory open?" he asked. "I could sure use something to eat." I told him it was not. "Do you know any place else I can get some food?" he asked. I thought about my cold cuts, my vegetables. I thought about inviting a strange man to my room.

"No," I said. "I'm sorry. I don't."

"That's all right," he said, draining his cup. "I'll just have another one of these." So I said goodbye to him and left him there, feeding his nickels into the machine.

Halfway up the stairs to the library, it occurred to me that I could *bring* him a sandwich, and I ran back down to the Red Table Cafe to tell him so, but he was gone. I ran down the length of the hall, checking empty classrooms. I opened the door at the end of the hallway and checked the quadrangle. I even checked the chapel, but he was gone. In less than thirty seconds, the man with the blue eyes had utterly vanished, and it was only then that I had the strange feeling that I knew who he was—the hungry one I did not feed, the thirsty one I gave no drink.

"Who do you claim to be?" the Jews ask Jesus. They cannot see the mountain because they are standing on it. "If I glorify myself, my glory is nothing," he answers them, explaining why he cannot answer them. He cannot do it for them. He cannot do it for himself. Only God can glorify him in God's own good time. And until that time he roams among us, the troublesome stranger in our midst. "So they picked up stones to throw at him, but Jesus hid himself and went out of the temple."

As far as I can tell, he still hides himself. He is an elusive stranger. Sometimes it is possible to identify him before he gets away, but most of the time you only know him after he is gone, like the drifter who wants to tell you his story only you do not have time, so you hand him a dollar and walk away. Or the woman with the tear-stained face who disappears while you decide whether to ask her what is wrong; or the bewildered child whose mother scolds him for being alive and whose sorrowful eyes catch yours just as she drags him off the bus.

These are the strangers who lay claim to our hearts, although they make no claims for themselves. In their presence we fail them. It is only after they are gone that we know who they were. That is why it is so easy for us to sacrifice them. We did not know. How could we have known? Who expected him to show up looking like that?

The amazing thing is, Jesus never seems to blame us. He knows how it is, being human, and beyond that he seems to prefer traveling incognito. Maybe that is something else he knows about us: if we were always sure who he was and where he could be found, then we would stop looking for him in every face, in every place. We would stop searching for him at all and settle down for a nice long nap.

There is only one sure clue to his identity, according to John. "When you have lifted up the Son of Man, then you will know that I am." He is the one on the tree, the one who is always getting himself killed, because he cannot or will not defend himself against those who pick up rocks. Who does he claim to be? Yahweh in our midst, the hidden one, whose only crime is love. The one whom we recognize one moment after he has gone away.

Note

1. C. S. Lewis, *The Case for Christianity* (New York: Macmillan, 1989), 45.

Eleven

The Prophet Mary

Mary took a pound of costly perfume made of pure nard, anointed Jesus' feet, and wiped them with her hair. The house was filled with the fragrance of the perfume. But Judas Iscariot, one of his disciples (the one who was about to betray him), said, "Why was this perfume not sold for three hundred denarii and the money given to the poor?"

JOHN 12:3–5

THE DAY BEFORE HE ENTERED JERUSALEM FOR THE last time, Jesus stopped in to see his old friends Mary, Martha, and Lazarus in the suburb of Bethany. They were a family dear to his heart, two sisters and a brother who seemed to think of him as a brother, too. He loved them, John tells us, although he does not tell us why. Maybe there is never a "why" to love. They called him Lord, so they knew who he was, and yet they were not his disciples, or at least not in the formal sense. They were his friends, the three people in whose presence he could be a man as well as a messiah.

Just a short time ago Jesus had worked a miracle at their house. "Lord, he whom you love is ill," the sisters had written him, and he had crossed the Jordan to come to them, knowing full well it was too late. Then, after Jesus the *man* had wept in front of his friend's tomb, Jesus the *messiah* shouted him out of it and restored Lazarus to life.

Now he has returned to them with the chief priests hot on his trail. Chatting with Samaritan women is one thing and healing the blind on the Sabbath is another, but reviving corpses is something else altogether. By raising Lazarus from the dead, Jesus has made it to the top of the religious right's "most wanted" list. His days are numbered and he knows it. When he arrives at his friends' house in Bethany with his disciples, they can see it on his face.

So they take Jesus in and they care for him, shutting the world out for this one night at least. They make him supper, all of them chopping up things for the stew while he sits and watches them. Martha is in charge, of course. The others do what she tells them to do. Lazarus is still clumsy from his four days in the tomb, handling the paring knife like a tree saw and staring at the potato in his hand as if he had never seen one before. Martha notices this and gives him a wooden spoon instead. His job is to stir when she says stir.

Mary, meanwhile, has slipped away, gone to find something in her room. Martha is used to this. Mary is the moody one, who disappears sometimes even when she is sitting right there with everyone else. A certain look comes over her face as if she were listening to something no one else can hear. Martha knows there is nothing to be done about it but to work around her, being careful to reel her back in when she drifts too far.

Finally supper is on the table and they all sit down to eat, sharing their hopes and naming their fears. Lazarus sits near his friend, unaware that he himself is the cause of all this concern. A trade has occurred, and he does not even know it. Jesus was more or less safe as long as he stayed across the Jordan, beyond the reach of his enemies in Jerusalem, but by returning to Bethany to save his friend, he has signed his own death warrant. Practicing what he preaches, he has traded his life for the life of his friend, unless he can find a way to escape the net that is drawing in around him.

No one notices that Mary has gone again until she comes back, holding a slender clay jar in her hands. Without a word she kneels at Jesus' feet and breaks the neck of the jar, so that the smell of spikenard fills the room—a sharp scent somewhere between mint and ginseng. As everyone in the room watches her, she does four remarkable things in a row.

First she loosens her hair in a room full of men, which a respectable woman never does. Then she pours balm on Jesus' feet, which also is not done. The head, maybe, but not the feet. Then she touches him, a single woman caressing the feet of a rabbi—also not done, not even among friends—and then she wipes the salve off again with her hair. It is totally inexplicable, the bizarre end to an all around bizarre act.

Most of us are so moved by the scene that we overlook these eccentricities, or else we do not care about them. The point is that she loved him, right? But we also tend to confuse this account with the other three in the Bible—one each from Matthew, Mark, and Luke. In the first two, the woman who anoints is an unnamed woman at Simon the Leper's house who pours nard on Jesus' head, and in the third she is a sinner, a woman of the night who washes his feet with her tears and covers them with kisses before rubbing them with oil of myrrh.

Only in John's account does the woman have a name—Mary—and a relationship with Jesus. She is not a stranger, not a sinner, but his longtime friend—which makes her act all the more peculiar. He knows she loves him. He loves her too. So why this public demonstration, this odd pantomime in front of all their friends? It is extravagant. It is excessive. She has gone overboard, as Judas is quick to note.

"Why was this ointment not sold for three hundred denarii

and the money given to the poor?" That is what he wants to know. A day laborer and his family could live a year on that much money, and here she has blown it all on your feet, for God's sake. It reminds me of those wine auctions you read about in the newspaper sometimes—fabulously old bottles of Chateau Lafitte Rothschild discovered in some castle cellar, sold for thousands, even millions of dollars. These treasures are not bought to be drunk, however. They are bought to be kept and admired, maybe sold again—precious substances to be saved, not used. Heaven forbid that anyone should uncork one and pour it out, not even for the Last Supper.

"Leave her alone," Jesus says, brushing all objections aside. "She bought it so that she might keep it for the day of my burial. You always have the poor with you, but you do not always have me." Now that is about as odd a thing to say as anything Mary did. Here is the champion of the poor, who makes a regular practice of putting their needs ahead of his own, suddenly pulling rank. Leave her alone. Leave me alone. You will have the poor to look after until the end of time. Just this once, let her look after me, because my time is running out.

Whatever Mary thought about what she did, and whatever anyone else in the room thought about it, Jesus knew it was a message from God—not the hysteric ministrations of an old maid gone sweetly mad but the careful act of a prophet. Everything around her smacked of significance. Judas, the betrayer, challenging her act. The flask of nard—wasn't it left over from Lazarus' funeral? Out in the yard, a freshly vacated tomb that still smelled of burial spices, waiting for a new occupant. The air was dense with death, and while there may at first have been some doubt about whose death it was, Mary's prophetic act revealed the truth.

She was anointing Jesus for his burial, and while her behavior may have seemed strange to those standing around, it was no stranger than that of the prophets who went before her, like Ezekiel, who ate the scroll of the Lord as a sign that he carried the word of God around inside of him, or Jeremiah, who smashed the clay jar to show God's judgment on Judah and Jerusalem, or Isaiah, who walked around Jerusalem naked and barefoot as an oracle against the nations. Prophets do these things. They act out. They act out the truth that no one else can see, and those who stand around watching either write them off as crazy or fall silent before the disturbing news they bring from God.

When Mary stood before Jesus with that pound of pure nard, for a moment—just one moment—it could have gone either way. She could have anointed his head and everyone there could have proclaimed him a king. But she did not do that. When she moved toward him, she dropped to her knees and poured the salve on his feet, which could mean only one thing. The only man who got his feet anointed was a dead man, and Jesus knew it. "Leave her alone," he said to those who would have prevented her. "Leave her alone."

So Mary proceeded to rub his feet with ointment so precious that its sale might have fed a poor family for a year, an act so lavish that it suggests another layer to her prophecy. There will be nothing prudent or economical about the death of this man, just as there has been nothing prudent or economical about his life. In him, the extravagance of God's love is made flesh. In him, the excessiveness of God's mercy is made manifest.

This bottle will not be held back to be kept and admired. This precious substance will not be saved. It will be opened, offered, and used, at great price. It will be raised up and poured out for all humankind, emptied to the last drop. How will it happen? When will it happen? Can anything be done? No one in the room knows the answers to those questions yet. The storm is still brewing in the distance, but Mary has given them the forecast. It will be bad, very bad, but that is no reason to lock up their hearts and head for the cellar. Whatever they need, there will be enough to go around, for there is nothing frugal about the love of God, or about the lives of those who serve him.

Mary got the message and acted on it. While some of those standing by thought her mad, or smitten, or (God forbid) wasteful, at least she and the one whose feet she rubbed suspected the truth. Where God is concerned, there is no need to fear running out—of nard or of life, either one. Where God is concerned, there is always more—more than we can either ask or imagine—gifts from our lavish, lavish Lord.

✒ *Deep in Christ's Bones*

Twelve

Clothed with Power

When the day of Pentecost had come, they were all together in one place. And suddenly from heaven there came a sound like the rush of a violent wind, and it filled the entire house where they were sitting.

ACTS 2:1—2

IF YOU BELIEVE THE BIBLE, THEN THERE IS NO BETTER proof that Jesus was who he said he was than the before-and-after pictures of the disciples. Before Pentecost, they were dense, timid bumblers who fled at the least sign of trouble. Afterwards, they were fearless leaders. They healed the sick and cast out demons. They went to jail gladly, where they sang hymns until the walls fell down. How did this transformation occur? You can read all about it in the book of Acts.

The last thing Jesus told his disciples to do before he ascended into heaven was to go back to Jerusalem and wait there for God's promise to come true. They would be baptized by the Holy Spirit, he told them, and they would be clothed with power from on high (Luke 24:49). With little or no idea what any of that meant, they did as they were told. They went back to Jerusalem—not to the temple but to an ordinary room in an ordinary house—and there they waited, along with the women who had come with them, including Jesus' mother and his brothers (Acts 1:14).

For the most part they prayed while they waited, and I expect at least some of them were asking God to tell them a little bit about what they were waiting for. How would they know when the power had fallen on them? Would it tingle? Would it hurt? How did the Holy Spirit go about baptizing people, exactly? Jesus had said something about fire, which sounded dangerous. Did he mean real fire or spiritual fire? Maybe they should fill some jars with water just in case things got out of hand.

They did not have to wait long for the answer to their prayers. On the day of Pentecost, a Jewish festival set fifty days after Passover, they were all together in one place when they got a crash course in power. First there was wind, then there was fire, then they were filled with the Holy Spirit and overflowed with strange languages: one spoke Parthian while another spoke Latin, and two others found their tongues curling around the exotic sounds of Egyptian and Arabic.

They may not have known what they were saying, but the crowd they drew did. Devout Jews from all over the world stood in the doorways and windows, listening to a bunch of Galileans tell about the power of God in their own tongues so that no one was left out. The Holy Spirit turned out to be a phenomenal linguist, whom everyone present could understand.

And still it baffled them all, the speakers as well as the listeners. They were in the grips of something that bypassed reason and some of them could not bear it, so they started hunting for a reason. "They are filled with new wine," someone said (drunk, in other words), but Peter said no, it was only nine o'clock in the morning—meaning, I suppose, that if it had been later in the day drunk might have been a real possibility.

Then he got up and delivered a sensational sermon, based on the second chapter of Joel. "In the last days," he proclaimed, quoting Joel quoting God, "I will pour out my Spirit upon all flesh, and your sons and your daughters shall prophesy, and your young men shall see visions, and your old men shall dream dreams." That is what is happening now, Peter tells them. The Holy Spirit of God is being poured out on them and this is how it looks: wind like the wind that revived the valley of dry bones, and fire like the fire that led Israel through the desert, and tongues like the tongues that erupted at Babel, but in reverse this time. At Babel, God confused human speech so that people could not understand each other anymore; at Pentecost, God reverses the curse. What sounds like babble is intelligible speech—better yet, is gospel—and everyone present understands it.

According to Acts, three thousand people were baptized that day. It was a miracle. It was the birthday of the Christian church, when a dozen bumblers received power from on high and proceeded to turn the world upside down. What happened in that room spread from Jerusalem to Athens to Rome to Alexandria. It spread across nations, across centuries, across cultures as far removed from Israel as we are from the moon. Because of what happened in that room, people who do not speak a word of Hebrew have come to believe in a Hebrew Lord, who is worshiped today in every language on earth.

It happened by the power of the Holy Spirit, which the Bible talks about in at least two ways. First, as the abiding presence of God in Christ, with all the safety and comfort that relationship promises. This is the Spirit most of us know and love—the Spirit of peace and concord—the one that smooths our ruffled feathers and revives our weary souls, the one that—lo!—is with us always, whenever we have the good sense to breathe in and say thank you.

But there is another way the Spirit acts—not another spirit but another manifestation of the same Spirit—that is not nearly so comforting. This is the Spirit who blows and burns, howling down the chimney and turning all the lawn furniture upside down. Ask Job about the whirlwind, or Ezekiel about the chariot of fire. Ask anyone who was in that room on Pentecost what it was like to be caught up in the Spirit, and whether it is something they would like to happen *every* Sunday afternoon.

When I was in Memphis awhile back I had a Sunday off, so I went as far from the Episcopal Church as I could go. I went to Al Green's Full Gospel Tabernacle, where the service begins at eleven and ends around two. There was a huge choir, a three-piece band, and a sound system turned all the way up. There was a church about half-full of people, who drifted in during the first thirty minutes of the service. Sunday school attendance was announced, the collection was taken, and the music began to build—listless at first, then gathering volume and focus until the service was in full swing.

For three full hours, we sang and clapped and raised our hands in the air. Children stood stomping their feet on the pews or crawled around underneath them while their mothers praised God and danced in place. Different members of the choir stepped forward to sing solos, as the band changed tempo to match each one's style. All of the songs had pounding rhythms that built and built until people began to be slain in the spirit. One woman right in front of me bolted from her pew and ran around the perimeter of the church twice, while another one nearer the front stood up and did a jerking dance until she fell on the floor. An usher threw a white sheet over her so that her petticoat would not show, and several members of the church knelt around her until her convulsions stopped.

I felt like I was caught in the middle of a thunderstorm, so I did what you are supposed to do: I made myself very small and held perfectly still. Lightning did not strike me, which was an answer to my prayer, but in the months since then I have wondered about my reaction. Was it simply a reaction to that kind of worship or was it more than that? If I had been in that room on the first Pentecost day, would I have done the same thing? "Oh God, if you are about to pour out your Spirit and this is what it looks like, would you please skip me?"

Am I the only one? Who else wants an umbrella when it looks like the Spirit is about to start coming down with wind and with fire? "Only a fool would pray for the Holy Spirit," says Alan Jones, dean of the Episcopal Cathedral in San Francisco. "Only fools for Christ do," he goes on, suggesting that the Spirit is most present at three open spaces in our lives: "In the unpredictable, in the place of risk and in those areas over which we have no control."[1]

Which was where the disciples were. And that is where we are, more times that we would like to admit—not only as individuals but also as members of this body that was born two thousand years ago. It is no crime to pray for the gentle Spirit at such times—to ask God to restore predictability, to remove us from risk, to give us back the comfortable illusion of control that helps us sleep at night.

But Pentecost is our reminder that there is another side to God's Spirit—one that can set us on fire, transform our lives, turn the world upside down. It is not predictable. It is very risky and it is beyond our control, but one thing we *can* do is fold our umbrellas and put them away. If we want to be fools for Christ, that is. If we want to be clothed with power from on high.

Note

1. "Pentecost: Pursued by the Spirit," *Episcopal Life* (June 1992).

Thirteen

Cut to the Heart

Now when they heard this, they were cut to the heart and said to Peter and to the other apostles, "Brothers, what should we do?"

ACTS 2:37

TUNE INTO THE SECOND CHAPTER OF ACTS, AND you can hear the first real sermon Peter ever preached. He preached it in Jerusalem, about fifty days after Jesus' execution. During those fifty days, Jesus appeared to Peter and the other disciples a number of times—clearly alive after his death, the same but different. He had breathed on them, forgiven them, given them things to do. He had also eaten with them more than once, reminding them of the last time they had all sat down to supper together before he died.

He had been the host at that supper, in more ways than one. He ordered the food. He was the food. First his friends watched him as he took the bread, thanked God for it and broke it into pieces. "This is my body," he said to them as he passed it around, which must have shut them right up. Then he said the same sort of thing over the cup. "This cup that is poured out for you is the new covenant in my blood" (Luke 22:20).

If he had said, "Take, understand," no one could have done it, but he did not say that. He said, "Take, eat," so they did, and from that moment on it was the main way they remembered him.

Whenever they sat down to eat together, wherever they sat down, he was there. They could not take a bite of bread or a swallow of wine without hearing his voice in their ears. So they ate together a lot because they needed all the help they could get in figuring out how to live their new lives. Easter had changed everything for them. They had felt God's fire on their heads and God's wind in their faces. They were all different. Things they had been afraid of before did not frighten them anymore. They had found new strength in themselves, new wisdom they never knew they had.

The problem was how to translate all this newfound voltage into a way of life that would last. Otherwise Easter would remain a one-time event that involved no more than a handful of people. What Peter and the others had to do was turn the Easter story into an Easter community whose life together would be a sign of Christ's ongoing life in the world. If you listen carefully, you can hear all this going on in Peter's sermon—Peter, who of all the disciples had been most prone to saying crazy, impulsive things, suddenly sounding like an archangel, speaking so eloquently of Jesus' life and death that those who listened to him were cut to the heart. "Brothers," they said to him and the others, "what should we do?"

If you have ever been cut to the heart yourself, then you know how they felt. Every now and then, if you are really, really lucky, you hear something so right and true that it pierces through all your defenses and goes straight to your heart. It can make you drop to your knees. It can make you laugh until you cry, or cry until you laugh, but it is not a mental thing at all. It is a physical thing that requires a physical response. You have to *do* something about it, and sometimes you need help figuring out what that is. "What should we do?" the Israelites asked Peter, and he did not even stop to think.

"Repent, and be baptized every one of you in the name of Jesus Christ," he said, "so that your sins may be forgiven; and you will receive the gift of the Holy Spirit." I wish like anything that I could hear what Peter told them with new ears, but I am afraid that his heart-felt answer to his heart-struck listeners has become something of a formula in our own time. Maybe that is all we know how to do with something that powerful: get it under control again. Encase it in plastic. Turn it into a three-step procedure that must be done in the right order with the right words or else it won't work.

The way I was taught it, to repent means to get down on your knees and tell God what a miserable sinner you are, and then to ask Jesus into your heart. To be baptized means to be sprinkled or dunked in a public ceremony so that other people know you are serious about this, and then to start going to that church. You have to check this out carefully, however, since what counts for baptism in one church may not count in another. To receive the Holy Spirit is to complete the process, but again this differs from church to church. In some, it means inhaling God's own life-giving breath any way that comes. For others, it means very specific things like speaking in tongues.

But still, that is the basic procedure, and it has worked plenty well for plenty of people. I just cannot believe that it was what Peter had in mind. His world had just been turned upside down. He had just had all his doors blown off their hinges and when the Israelites asked him, "What should we do?" I do not believe he gave them a three-step prescription to fill. I believe he told them how to prepare for a holy hurricane.

"Reorient your lives." That is the truth of what he told them, knowing full well that was what would happen the moment Jesus came to live in them. Forget everything you ever thought you knew about who is in charge in this world. Get ready to revise all your notions about what makes someone great, or right, or worthy of your attention. If you think you know which way is up, think again. If you think you know how things should turn out in the end, get ready to be wrong. This Jesus I have been telling you about is one surprise after another. You cannot second-guess him. All you can do is love him and let him love you back, any way he sees fit. Sometimes it is so strong it can scare you to death. You want to know what you should do? Repent, return, revise, reinvent yourself.

Then go get born again, by water and the Spirit. Walk into the river of death with him. Go under with him, and while you are down there let the current carry away everything that stands between you and him. Then, when all your own breath is gone, let him give you some of his. Take his breath inside of you. Let it save your life, and when he rises, rise with him, understanding that your life is no longer your own. You died down there. You are borrowing his life now. Let someone make the sign of the cross on your forehead to remind you of that, and join the community of those who call themselves his body, because they believe his heart beats in every one of them.

Then receive the Holy Spirit. That is, breathe. Deeply. Receive your life as a gift invisible as air, and prepare to be astonished by all the forms that breath can take. Under the power of the Holy Spirit, shy people have been known to step up onto platforms and say audacious things. Cautious people have become daredevils, frugal people have become philanthropists and people who used to be as sour as dill pickles have become rich with friends.

There is no limit to what the Holy Spirit can do. You just cannot hold your breath, that's all. You have to keep breathing, keep paying attention, keep responding to whatever crazy idea you come up with next. Some people call it intuition. Others call it inspiration. Forever and ever, the church has called it Holy Spirit.

That is Peter's answer to those who want to know what they should do in response to the Easter story. Repent. Be baptized.

Receive the Holy Spirit. Then and now, that is how the Easter story gets translated into an Easter way of life that will last. That is how we experience the risen Christ, even if we never saw or heard him in the flesh. For further details, see the book of Acts.

About three thousand people were baptized as a result of Peter's sermon. That is some altar call. Afterwards, they devoted themselves to the apostles' teaching and fellowship, to the breaking of bread, and to the prayers. They held all their property in common, so that no one had more than anyone else. They broke bread at each other's homes and ate their food with glad and generous hearts, praising God and having the goodwill of all the people. "And day by day, the Lord added to their number those who were being saved."

If it sounds like a fairy tale, it isn't. It is what happens when you-know-who is around. Every time we break bread together he is with us, not because we invited him but because he invited us. He is the host. He ordered the food and he is the food, the breath, the life. What should we do? Taste and see.

Fourteen

How Not to Hinder God

Then Peter began to speak to them: "I truly understand that God shows no partiality, but in every nation anyone who fears him and does what is right is acceptable to him."

ACTS 10:34–35

N O ONE WAS MORE SURPRISED THAN PETER WHEN these words fell out of his mouth. At the time he was standing in the living room at the home of Cornelius the centurion, an officer in the Roman army that occupied Judea. According to Luke, Cornelius was one of the good guys, well regarded by the whole Jewish nation. He had even become a God-fearer, someone who believed in Israel's God, although as a Gentile he kept a certain distance. He was not circumcised and he did not observe Jewish dietary laws, which was one of the main reasons why Jews and Gentiles did not eat together.

There were some Jews who believed Gentiles were just plain filthy, hopelessly immoral and prone to idolatry, but other Jews gave them the benefit of the doubt and lived with them in harmony. They simply could not eat together, that was all, because as hard as they tried, Gentiles might slip up and put some pork in the beans, or thicken a veal stew with milk.

I wish there were some way we could understand how important dietary law has been to the people of Israel. Most of us have eaten bacon all our lives, and we do not think twice about combining milk and meat, but if we were first-century Jews, the very thought would make us break out in a cold sweat. It would be like coming to church one morning to find pork chops and scotch whiskey on the altar instead of bread and wine. What's the difference? Food is food!

But God told us to do it another way, and we have been doing it that way for as long as anyone can remember. It is in the Bible that way: "Do this in remembrance of me." Bread and wine, not pork chops and scotch. We would not be who we are if we ate pork chops and drank scotch in church.

If that does not help you understand the dietary issue, imagine anything that, for you, is the dividing line between Christians and other people—the one thing that makes us who we are, that is not negotiable, that we cannot let slide without letting slide our whole identity as people of God. And when you have figured out what that is, get ready to let it go, because that is what Peter did. He had to. God gave him a vision that changed everything he had ever believed about who he was and how he was supposed to live.

This Peter is the same Simon Peter whom we know from the gospels, Jesus' first disciple—the first to step out on the water toward him, the first to confess his true identity, the first to betray him and, after his death, the first to let Gentiles into the Christian church even though it was the farthest thing from his mind. Here is how it happened, according to the book of Acts.

Peter was staying in Joppa, a seaport that is now a suburb of Tel Aviv. Cornelius was in Caesarea, the seat of the Roman government, about forty miles up the coast. God was in between them, arranging the visions that would bring them together. Cornelius' dream came first. It was about three in the afternoon when an angel came into his room, clear as day, and told him first of all that Cornelius was a good man, whose alms and prayers pleased God very much. Then the angel told him to send some of his men to Joppa, to the house by the sea where Peter was staying.

The next day about noon, as those men were approaching the city, Peter went up on the roof of the house to pray. While he was there he got hungry and sent for something to eat, but while it was still cooking he had a vision of his own—much stranger than Cornelius'—in which heaven opened and something like a large sheet came down, lowered to the ground by its four corners. When Peter looked inside it, he saw every kind of forbidden creature—camels, badgers, buzzards, bats, crocodiles, lizards, a pig—all the things on the "don't eat" list in Leviticus 11, enough to make a good Jewish man lose his appetite or worse.

Then Peter heard a voice say, "Get up, Peter; kill and eat." You or I might have thought it was the devil talking, but Peter seemed to recognize the voice. "By no means, Lord," he said, "for I have never eaten anything that is profane or unclean." It reminds me of the time Jesus tried to wash his feet and Peter said, "You will never wash my feet." Peter was stubborn, which may have been why God had to say all the important things to him three times.

"What God has made clean, you must not call profane," the voice said back. This happened three times, and then the sheet was hauled back into heaven.

So when Cornelius' men arrived shortly after that and told him they were there because of a vision too, Peter began to put two and two together. He went back with them to Caesarea where Cornelius met him and took him into his house, which was full of Cornelius' relatives and close friends. This took Peter aback. He had prepared himself to meet one Gentile, not a whole house full of them. "You yourselves know that it is unlawful for a Jew to associate with or to visit a Gentile." That is the first thing Peter said to them, and I imagine some of them were crushed. Here they had waited for this great man whom Cornelius had told them so much about and he turned out to be just like all the rest, treating them as if they were dirty and he might catch something just by being in the same room with them.

"But . . ." he said next. I love that word. Sometimes I think the whole gospel swings on that word ("I was lost but now I'm found, was blind but now I see"). It means things can change. It means we do not always know everything there is to know. It means God can still teach us something. "But," Peter said, "God has shown me that I should not call anyone profane or unclean. So when I was sent for, I came without objection. Now may I ask why you sent for me?"

Cornelius answered him, "All of us are here in the presence of God to listen to all that the Lord has commanded you to say." So Peter began by telling them what he had just learned for himself. "I truly understand that God shows no partiality, but in every nation anyone who fears him and does what is right is acceptable to him."

If anyone in that room breathed for a full minute after he said that, there was something wrong with them. Because Peter had just said something no one on earth had authorized him to say. He had just opened the church to those it had previously shut out, people with whom he was not even supposed to associate. He had not checked with anyone in Jerusalem first. He did not even quote a passage of scripture to back him up. He based what he said on the fresh revelation God had given him, and on his belief that Jesus Christ is Lord of all. Not some, but all.

While he was still speaking, the Holy Spirit fell on everyone in the room, both the Jews who were there with Peter and all of Cornelius' crowd. Everyone was speaking in tongues and praising God, so that Peter could hardly make himself heard. "Can anyone withhold the water for baptizing these people who have received the Holy Spirit just as we have?" he asked. And they were all baptized right then and there.

Peter got in big trouble for it, too. When he arrived back in Jerusalem, his Jewish brothers jumped all over him. Why had he gone to that house in the first place, they asked him? And what had possessed him to eat unclean food? From their perspective, Peter had sold out. He had crossed over the dividing line between God's people and other people. He had disobeyed the law, which was not negotiable, which was the one thing that made them who they were.

As gently as he could, Peter told them what had happened to him, how God had taken that one thing away from him but had given him something else instead—a vision that included all creatures, all people, whom God alone had the right to call clean or unclean. He had not sold out. He had traded up, and when he saw what happened at Cornelius' house he knew he was right.

"If then God gave them the same gift that he gave us when we believed in the Lord Jesus Christ," Peter said, "who was I that I could hinder God?" When he said that, everyone got very quiet. Then they praised God, saying, "Then God has given even to the Gentiles the repentance that leads to life."

How often, in the church, do we try to say where the Spirit may or may not blow, when the only thing God has asked us to do is to try and keep up with it wherever it goes?

Fifteen

The Shepherd's Flute

I am the good shepherd. The good shepherd lays down his life
for the sheep.

JOHN 10:11

L AST WEEK WHEN MY HUSBAND ED AND I WERE TALK-
ing about the difference between hired hands and owners,
he told me a story about the time he and his friend Tommy
Brannon went duck hunting on the Flint River. They had been
out all day in Tommy's boat, sharing equally in the care and pleasure of it, when it came time at last to pack up and go home.
Motoring back to the launch pad, they heaved the prow of the
boat up on the river bank and began to haul their guns and decoys
back to the car.

On their second trip back to the river, however, the boat was
gone. Looking downstream they saw it floating away, about ten
feet from the bank. So they dropped everything and ran after it,
crashing through the underbrush to draw even with it, but the
closer they got, the further it moved out into the main current of
the river—first ten feet, then twelve feet, then twenty feet away,
gaining speed as it went.

Finally came the moment of truth. As cold and tired as they
both were, it was clear that one of them would have to strip and
swim after the boat. They looked at each other and they both

knew who it would be. "It wasn't *my* boat," Ed said, but he helped out by cheering for Tommy as he tore off his camouflage jumpsuit and dove into the river.

"I am the good shepherd. The good shepherd lays down his life for the sheep." That is what makes him good, according to John—his willingness to get involved, to risk his life for the life of his flock. *His* flock. Not somebody else's flock, which he gets paid five dollars an hour to look after, but his own flock—the one he has bought and bred, doctored and protected. He is invested in it, in more ways than one.

His sheep are his livelihood, for one thing, but they are also his extended family. They know his voice, his touch, his walk. If they are grazing with a thousand other sheep and he calls them, they will separate themselves from the crowd and follow him home. His flute is the sound of safety for them—the sound of still waters and green pastures. He knows them too, by name and disposition: Houdini, who is always escaping through some hole in the fence; Pegleg, who limps from the time she stepped in a hole; Bossy, who likes nothing better than butting heads.

There is something about ownership that creates intimacy, especially ownership of living things. A dog or a cat can become a soul friend who knows how you are feeling when no one else does. I have a cat named Merlin who is my spiritual director. When I am frantic, he goes to sleep on my lap. When I am sad, he leaps out at me from dark corners and when I am fine he takes a break and goes off to do things on his own. Some people say we pick pets who look like us. If it is true, it is because they really are extensions of us, creatures who are so much a part of our lives that sometimes it is not easy to tell who owns whom.

Ownership is not just a matter of legal title, however. You have heard people talk about "owning their feelings" or "owning up to" a problem. When I hear expressions like that, and when

I put them together with the story of the good shepherd who owns the sheep, I begin to think of ownership as a certain kind of relationship, one that is created between people and other people, or animals, or things. Then ownership is not about mere possession, but about being bound to something beyond ourselves, about identifying with it so strongly that it becomes part of us. When it is threatened, we defend it as if we were defending our own bodies, and sometimes that can get us into trouble.

Someone I know was visiting a friend of his in California not too long ago. They met at the airport and as they were getting into the car to leave, my friend opened his door so wide that it whacked the sideview mirror of a red sports car parked next to it. There was no harm done, but the owner of the sports car happened to be sitting inside of it at the time, and when he heard the whack he exploded out the driver's door.

"What the hell do you think you're doing?" he yelled at my surprised friend, at which point *his* friend jumped out of the car and said, "Don't you talk to him like that! It was an accident, for crying out loud, and you can see for yourself that nothing's broken."

"I'm talking to him, not you, buster," the man said furiously.

"Yeah, well, when you're talking to him, you're talking to me," my friend's friend said, and the man backed down. Say what you will about brawls in airport parking lots, there is ownership in that statement. "When you're talking to him, you're talking to me." There is intimate relationship in that, full willingness to risk one's own safety in order to defend someone else's. Not because he cannot take care of himself, but because you care for him— you are connected to him, and you know it.

All in all, we are warned away from getting involved in other people's problems. Parents teach us to mind our own business and let other people mind theirs. Therapists call it "trespassing boundaries," or "codependence," and they have a point. Sometimes our ownership of others' problems ends up crippling both them and us, by eroding our responsibility for our own lives. When we make a habit of rescuing other people, we prevent them from learning about the consequences of their actions. We help them keep their illusions about themselves, and we get to be heroes in the bargain, but it is not good for them or for us. Everybody deserves a chance to fail. It is how we learn to be human.

But we also deserve to have someone in our lives who will say, "When you're talking to him, you're talking to me," someone who will tear her clothes off and dive into the water when what is disappearing down the river happens to be us. That is not "co-dependence." That is *agape*, self-giving love, the kind of love the good shepherd practices and the kind he teaches.

If the shepherd had been a hired hand, we would not even know his name. A hired hand would have taken one look at the wolf (or the river current, or the bully) and vanished. If he had been a religious hired hand, he might have said, "God bless you! I'll pray for you!" before he disappeared, but he would not have come to the rescue. Because a hired hand does not care for the sheep. He does not own them, involving himself so deeply in their lives that he risks his own to protect theirs. He minds his own business. He takes care of himself.

The good shepherd, on the other hand, lays down his life for the sheep. But then what happens to the sheep, you are wondering—who protects them after he is dead? Well, I will tell you. On the night before he died, they all fell asleep after a big meal, with the sound of the shepherd's flute in their ears. And as they slept, they shared a terrible dream: of wolves with clubs and torches who came out of the woods, led their shepherd away, and tore him to shreds on a hillside outside of town.

In the dream, they huddled for safety, unable to think, unable to move, and they stayed that way for three whole days, wondering if they would starve to death before the wolves came back to finish the job. But then on the third day, they heard a flute—far away at first, then drawing nearer—that woke them from their sleep, and they stood once again in the presence of their good shepherd.

Everything was the same again, but everything had changed. Looking around at each other, they saw what had happened. They had fallen asleep as sheep, but they had woken up as shepherds. As they slept, every one of them had been changed into the image of their master, and as they stood there staring at one another he handed them staves like his, and flutes, and sent them out to gather their own flocks. "Do for them as I did for you," he said, and played them a little tune as they set off to do just that.

Sixteen

Deep in Christ's Bones

*For just as the body is one and has many members, and all
the members of the body, though many, are one body, so it is
with Christ.*

I CORINTHIANS 12:12

THE DAY PAUL WAS INSPIRED TO COMPARE THE
church to a human body, he gave us an image of ourselves
that we are still growing into. It is a strong image, because each
of us is a body and we know what he is talking about. In order
to pick up a glass of grapefruit juice, it is not enough to have an
arm and four fingers. Without an opposable thumb you are lost.
Likewise, do not even think about walking with your inner ear
all messed up. It is not enough to have working legs and feet. You
need your inner gyroscope to tell you which way is up.

There are all kinds of things inside of us that we need without
thinking about them at all, at least not until one of them gets sick
and has to come out. Few of us get up in the morning and thank
God for our colons, our collarbones, or our mitochondria. We
do not even know the names of half the things that keep us alive,
but that does not bother them. They go right on keeping us alive
in spite of our alarming ignorance about them.

In general, we are happy to have two of everything we are
supposed to have two of and one of everything we are supposed

to have one of. More or less of any of these things tends to put us at a disadvantage, either physically or psychologically. Children born with too many parts or not enough of them are scheduled for surgery and those of us who lose parts of ourselves as adults find ways to live without them, but we rarely stop missing them. We have a built-in sense of wholeness that will not go away.

Paul knew he could get people's attention by talking about their bodies. Greek and Roman orators before him had used the same image to explore the nature of the state, so the church at Corinth was used to thinking metaphorically about the human body. What Paul and the politicians were all trying to do was to persuade people that what was true inside their own skin was also true outside of it, that wholeness was a matter of many different parts all being themselves and doing their jobs. Unity and diversity were not contradictory terms, in other words. They were two true words for one paradoxical reality, namely, that our survival depends not on our sameness but on our infinite variety.

Now that is fine when it is my liver or my kneecaps you are talking about. I rejoice in the difference between them and I would not want either of them trying to do the other's job. I count on all my parts to maintain their independence while they are working together, but the truth is that I do not think about them very much. It is all *me* in here, and I am largely unconscious of the intricate cooperation required to keep *me* alive.

The problem begins when you put me in community with a bunch of other people who look, smell, think, talk, and act differently from me. One is perfectly cheerful but she can talk for thirty minutes straight without stopping to breathe, while another has been so beaten up by life that everything he says comes out as a sneer. One speaks so intimately of God that everyone around her feels like a spiritual slouch, and another is a complete imposter who prays big hot air balloons on Sunday mornings and then goes home to knock his family around. "Now you are the body of Christ," Paul says, "and individually members of it."

I liked it better when we were talking about livers and knee-caps. Why? Because I do not handle the infinite variety outside of me nearly as well as I handle the infinite variety inside of me. Because other people challenge my established routines. I start doing something one way and suddenly I get lots of advice about doing it another way, or several other ways, until I lose my ap-petite for doing anything at all.

Do you know what I mean? You join a community looking for—what?—closeness, support, some measure of safety—and nine times out often what you get instead is this holy struggle to live and work with people who are just as angular as you are. The brains want everybody to act like brains and the hearts want everyone to act like hearts and there is always a hangnail who brings out the hangnail in everyone else.

In his book *The Company of Strangers*, Parker Palmer defines community as "that place where the person you least want to live with always lives!" And, he adds, when that person moves away someone else always arrives to fill the empty place. Most of us have a romantic notion of community that gets in our way, be-cause the real purpose of community is not to retreat someplace with other like-minded people, but to give ourselves up to the working of the Holy Spirit by learning how to live with people we may not like at all. What better way to open ourselves up to the God beyond our knowing than to begin with the neighbor beyond our knowing? What finer way to learn about the reconcil-ing power of Christ than to test it in a body of infinite variety?

One difficulty with Paul's metaphor, for me, is that I cannot feel it, not the way I can feel my own fingers and toes. He says that when one of us suffers we all suffer together, and when one of us is honored all the rest of us rejoice—but it does not seem to work that way very often. Oh, we may feel sorry for each other or glad for each other, but if someone hits you my skin does not bruise, and when you get a raise my standard of living does not go up. For all of Paul's good intentions and excellent theology, his metaphor really does not work. One member suffers and the vast majority do not even know about it, much less feel it. One member is honored and the rest of us may applaud, but we rarely experience the joy as if it were our own.

But what if Paul was not speaking metaphorically when he wrote about the body? What if he was speaking metaphysically instead—not making a comparison at all but stating a solid reality? He did not say, "You are *like* the body of Christ," after all. "You *are*," he said. "You *are* the body of Christ and individually members of it." Whether you realize it or not, whether you feel it or not. whether you like each other or not, you are the body of Christ and there is nothing you can do about it but act like it or not. The end.

Quantum physicists tell us that we have been living under the illusion of separateness for at least three hundred years now, ever since Sir Isaac Newton proposed that the universe worked like a great clock. According to his physics, the world is a collection of individual gears and springs that act in perfectly predictable ways. You can take them apart and put them back together again with no effect on the whole. To understand the clock, you need only understand the parts, which behave in regular and reasonable ways.

It was not until the discovery of subatomic reality earlier in this century that this illusion was dispelled. In fact, we learned, the universe behaves much more like a body than a clock. It is not possible to understand the parts without understanding the whole. We cannot even observe an electron without changing the way it acts, because we are all knit together in this invisible, unfathomable web of relationship. It has its own gorgeous order, but it is never entirely predictable, because every time a butterfly beats its wings in that web, every time a cat yawns or a baby sneezes, the whole web shifts to accommodate it. Quantum physicists call this chaos theory. Paul calls it the body of Christ—that great mystery of God that binds us together whether we know it, feel it, like it or not.

I got a chance to try all of this out recently, when the North Georgia Peace Council sponsored the ninth annual Martin Luther King Day walk through my hometown of Clarkesville. We are never a very big crowd but we are generally a pretty interesting one. This year we included folks from all the Main Street churches plus some Baha'is and Quakers and plain old humanists. The black Baptist preacher was there with his two little girls and so were some young people in t-shirts from Americorps, the new national service league devoted to caring for the developmentally disabled.

The plan was to walk from Grace-Calvary Episcopal Church to Mount Zion Baptist Church on the other side of the town square. That was easy enough, but just before we left we got word that the Ku Klux Klan was waiting for us at the square. This news rendered me somewhat breathless. There were plenty of police around, so it was not physical violence I feared. I feared my own reaction to people I had heard so much about all my life—people famous for their hatred, who called themselves Christians just like me. I think I feared for my soul—not only for what they might do to it, but for what I might do to it myself by returning their hate.

We set out, singing. The organizers of the walk always put the clergy at the front, which I had previously misinterpreted as an honor. This time I knew we were up there as buffers between those behind us and those ahead of us, human air bags in case of collision. For better or worse, we had an unobstructed view. We turned the corner, singing, "He's got the whole world in his hands," and there they were—several men and a woman in white robes and pointed hats, with some other people standing around them in plain clothes.

They did not hide their faces, which I appreciated. They just held up their signs so we could not miss them. One featured a picture of Dr. King's head with a rifle viewfinder zeroed in on it. "Our dream came true," it read. "James Earl Ray made our day," said another, and a third one proclaimed, "*Christ* is our King."

"He's got you and me, brother, in his hands." That is what we were singing as we turned the corner and walked away from them. "He's got you and me, sister, in his hands." I was not scared anymore. I was mystified, because if the song was right—if what Paul said is true—then I had just walked past some members of my own body, who were as hard for me to accept as a cancer or a blocked artery. And yet if I did not accept them—if I let them remain separate from me the way they wanted me to—then I became one of them, one more of the people who insist that there are some people who cannot belong to the body.

Actually, my struggle was irrelevant at that point, because if the song is right—if what Paul said is true—then God is not waiting for any of us to decide who is in or out of Christ's body, not even ourselves. This truth is beyond our consent or liking. We are the body of Christ and individually members of it. Whenever anyone laughs, cries, lives, or dies in this web of creation we are all affected by it whether we know it or not. When one suffers we all suffer and when one is honored all the rest of us rejoice, if only way down deep in Christ's bones where only he knows it is happening at all.

Most of the time we live as though this were a fond illusion, but there is a distinct possibility that it is our separateness which is the illusion instead. There is an old Sufi saying that goes like this: "You think because you understand *one* you must understand *two*, because one and one make two. But you must also understand *and*."

You know who our "and" is, don't you? The creator of all our parts, the author of our wholeness, the lover of complete impostors, the Lord of electrons, the one who's got the whole world in his hands with room left over, turning you and me and them into us.

Seventeen

The Silence of Angels

In the days of King Herod of Judea, there was a priest named Zechariah, who belonged to the priestly order of Abijah. His wife was a descendant of Aaron, and her name was Elizabeth.

LUKE 1:5

L UKE BEGINS HIS GOSPEL WITH TWO CHARACTERS you almost never hear about in church because they only come up at Christmastime, when everyone else is rushing on to Bethlehem. But according to Luke, the story of Jesus begins way, way before the night of the bright star. It begins with Zechariah and Elizabeth, who were the parents of the one who would announce the one who was to come.

They started out a barren old couple, both descendants of Aaron, both raised in priestly families to serve the temple in Jerusalem. In another time they might have been a clergy couple, but in their own time it was only Zechariah who went into the family business. Elizabeth's job was to have priestly children, only she didn't, and in her day all the blame fell on her. She was barren, as good as dead, and Zechariah could have divorced her for it.

He did not divorce her, however. Both of them were righteous, Luke tells us. Both of them lived blamelessly before the Lord, which means that they shared something as important as children—a way of life that bound them together as surely as getting up for midnight feedings or taking turns with the bed-time bath. When it was time for Zechariah to serve his week in Jerusalem, Elizabeth did not hang on to him. Her father and her father's father had done the same thing. Whether or not she went with Zechariah in body, she went with him in spirit, and what he did there he did for her as well.

The story Luke tells us turned out to be the most impor-tant day in both their lives. When Zechariah's section reported for duty that day, they cast lots to see who would do what and Zechariah got the prize. He alone would enter the sanctuary to burn incense on the holy altar, while the whole assembly of the people prayed outside. The smoke he produced would carry those prayers to God, perfuming them as they rose. Then Zechariah alone would emerge from the sanctuary to bless the people, rep-resenting God to them as he had represented them to God.

It was a job no priest could do twice in his lifetime and some never got to do it at all. It was as close as Zechariah would ever get to the Holy of Holies and still he was terrified when an angel appeared to him inside. *What did he expect?* Maybe he was con-centrating so hard on what he was doing that he forgot whose living room he was in. Or maybe he suffered from the curse of the professionally religious, who are so often frightened when God interrupts their routines.

If you ask me, he was scared because he was thinking about Elizabeth instead of the incense. "Do not be afraid, Zechariah," the angel told him, "for your prayer has been heard." Which prayer was that? Not a prayer for the people, on that day of all days, but a prayer for a child of his own. It was going to happen, the angel told him. It was such a sure thing that the miracle already had a name: John. Then the angel went into glorious detail about all that child would be and do. "Joy and gladness," the angel said, "spirit and power," but Zechariah held back.

"How will I know that this is so?" he asked the terrible angel. "For I am an old man and my wife is getting on in years." It was an awful moment, one of those thudding *faux-pas* that make you wish you could start over again, like when your beloved gives you the very present you asked for and the first thing you say is, "How much did that cost?"

"How will I know that this is so?" The commentaries call Zechariah's question the sin of disbelief, but I wonder about that. You might also call it a failure of imagination, a fear of disappointment, a habit of hopelessness. He had waited a long time for something that was systematically denied him. He had gotten used to not being heard. How was he supposed to know that this time would be different?

"I am Gabriel," the angel answered him. That is how you will know. Then, because Zechariah did not believe the good news, the angel silenced him, so when he emerged from the sanctuary on that day of all days he could not even finish doing his job. The people who had waited for a blessing went home without one, while Zechariah played a lonely game of charades on the temple steps. The religious professional could not speak, because an angel had silenced him.

Wherever this story is told, Zechariah's muteness is treated as his punishment for doubt. Because he could not say something nice he was not allowed to say anything at all. Or, more to the point, because he could not get with the program he was excluded from it. But he was not excluded from it. He remained essential to it. He may not have been able to speak when he got home but he was perfectly able to do something else, and it was not long before Elizabeth conceived. As the quiet months passed, her swelling belly gave him the proof the angel would not and when the child was born both his mother and his father agreed that his name was John.

Zechariah could do it, but he could not talk about it. It seems entirely possible to me that his silence was the angel's gift to him—an enforced sabbatical, a gestation period of his own during which the seeds of hope were sown again in his hushed soul. He could not learn anything with his mouth open. Nothing he could say held a candle to what was happening right in front of him, and his muteness turned out to be the wilderness in which his dream was born.

I like to think of Zechariah as the patron saint of the twenty-first-century church. Like him, we have been waiting a long time for our prayers to be heard. "Christ has died. Christ is risen. Christ will come again," we say over and over again. But where is he, exactly, and how much longer must we wait? It is hard to know what to say when people ask us where God is. Have faith? Be patient? Prayer works? Our words have gotten as old and tired as we have, and in many cases people have stopped believing us. They ask us the same thing Zechariah asked his angel. "How will we know that this is so?" Maybe it is time for us to claim the angel's gift of silence again—to stop talking so much, to stop trying to explain, to shut our own mouths before the terrible mystery of God and see what the quiet has to teach us.

I am not proposing that the church go mute, but I am wondering if it is not time for us to explore the idea that less is more. Our age is an age of bombardment, in which the zoom lens brings us face-to-face with more grief than most of us can bear. We are bombarded with images; we are also bombarded with words. It is always rush hour on the information highway. Each day feeds our addiction to data, to analysis, to the tantalizing illusion that someone can tell us what is really going on.

Meanwhile, very few words come at us without some hidden purpose. Words are used to win our votes, to change our minds, to empty our wallets. Words promise us things they cannot deliver and pretend to know things no one can know. There is no longer much correlation between word and truth. Each of us reserves the right to wait and see for ourselves. "How will I know that this is so?"

What would happen in a world like this if Christians were to become very still and quiet, creating oases of silence for people whose ears ache and whose heads hurt from all the noise? What would happen if we stopped pretending we could read God's mind and just sat down somewhere to do nothing together, watching out for whatever new thing God is doing next? What if, when we did speak, we committed ourselves to telling the truth, the whole truth and nothing but the truth, including all the things that we do not and can never know about God? What if we believed that silence is a virtue, pleasing to God?

Rabbi Lawrence Kushner has written a book called *God Was in This Place & I, i Did Not Know*. In it, he evokes the temple in Jerusalem—not Herod's temple, the one Zechariah served, but Solomon's temple—God's first house on earth. According to I Kings 6, the room was empty except for a throne that was also empty. Two golden cherubim spread their wings over it, facing each other across the mercy seat. Once a year their solitude was broken, when the high priest came to make amends for the people on the day of atonement. Inside that room, he had only one job: to utter the sacred name of God. The problem was, God's name was all written in vowels and no one knew how to pronounce it. No one was even allowed to try. As the high priest breathed in and out he could hear the sacred name on his lips. Yah-weh. I am who I am. I will be who I will be. God's perfect privacy and freedom, confessed with every human breath.

"Creation has at its center an empty throne in an empty room in which the unpronounceable Name is spoken once a year. And the sound of its name is the sound of breathing!" Kushner adds a pungent detail to the story. Before the high priest goes into the presence of the Lord, the other priests tie a rope around his leg, so that if he is struck dead inside they can haul him out without risking destruction themselves.[1]

We, meanwhile, crawl right into God's lap and start asking, "Why?" Perhaps Jesus himself has emboldened us, calling God "Abba" and telling us not to fear. But there is still room for reverence. There are still times to leave even the right things unsaid so that the silence resounds.

Zechariah learned the hard way. He could not speak until all the angel promised him had come true. Our own silence is voluntary, such as it is, a waiting and watching that will settle for nothing less than the truth. It may turn out to be, once again, the wilderness in which the dream is born, the utter quiet that opens the way to the night of the bright star.

Note

1. Kushner. God Was in This Place & I, i Did Not Know (Woodstock, Vt: Jewish Lights Publishing, 1991), 97.

Chickens and Foxes

Eighteen

Owning Your Own Shadow

Then he called the crowd again and said to them, "Listen to me, all of you, and understand: there is nothing outside a person that by going in can defile, but the things that come out are what defile."

MARK 7:14–15

R ECENTLY I HEARD ABOUT A CRANKY OLD PROFES-
sor who had a cranky old dog. During the warmer months he kept the dog at home, where it could spend at least part of the time outdoors. But when winter came he put the dog in a kennel because the animal went stir crazy inside, chewing things and ruining the carpets. While the dog was away, the professor was worse than ever, snapping at his family and ordering them around. When the dog returned home in the spring, things im-proved. The old man started kicking the dog again and stopped taking his ire out on everyone else.

It is an awful story, but everyone knows deep down inside how nice it is to have a scapegoat—someone you can blame for all the things you do not want to blame yourself for, someone who will carry your dark side for you so that you do not have to carry it yourself. That is why it is so helpful to keep an enemy or two on hand. As long as you can despise someone else for her meanness or his crookedness, you do not have to own up to any of those things in yourself. The target stays out there, where you can keep shooting at it, which keeps your mind off the target inside you, buried way back among all those other things stored in the garage of your heart.

Often, when we are reading the Bible, Pharisees and scribes perform this function for us. They make great targets. They are the nit-picking legalists who reject Jesus' teaching because he keeps breaking their rules. They are the holier-than-thou hypocrites who would rather be right than redeemed. Scripture helps us with these stereotypes by calling them blind guides, whitewashed tombs, snakes, a brood of vipers—all because they refused to believe the good news that their rules and their righteousness were no longer necessary, and they could trade all that in on a whole-hearted relationship with Jesus, also known as the Christ.

The scribes and Pharisees did not buy it. They had been following their rules a long time—both the written Torah, given to them directly by Moses, and the oral Torah, developed by faithful rabbis over hundreds of years. Between the two sets of laws, every aspect of human life on earth was set under God's will. There was nothing—not the least exchange between two people, not the simplest of meals—that was not covered by the law. Everything that could be done could be done in a holy way, and no one was more devoted to living that holiness than the Pharisees.

They were lay people, not priests, but they adopted priestly standards for themselves. They observed the sabbath reverently. They tithed everything, right down to the spices they put in their food. They ate every meal in a state of purity equal to that of the priests eating in the temple, because their homes *were* their temples and they cut themselves no slack.

So while we may criticize them sometimes for rejecting our good news, they were not bad people. On the contrary, they were some of the best people around—serious about their faith, concerned about their purity, devoted to pleasing God by living the most honorable lives they knew how. Chances are that every one of us has a Pharisee somewhere on our personal list of saints. Take away the label and maybe you can remember that person—someone whose obedience to God seemed as natural as air, although you know now how hard it must have been; someone whose quiet, steady virtue was like a light on a foggy night for you. Just seeing it helped you find your way. If that person could do it, so could you. That person raised the standard of what was possible for you, simply by the way he or she lived.

That is how it was with the Pharisees. They kept to very high standards, which would have been all right if that had helped them stay in communion with other people, but it tended to work the other way around, by cutting them off. Fully two-thirds of the oral Torah was about eating—what you could and could not eat, with whom, on what kind of dishes, out of what kind of pots. Some of the concerns were practical; hands were silverware in the ancient world and you did not want to share your babaganoush with someone who had just come in from trimming his sheep's hooves, not unless he washed first.

More of the concerns were spiritual, however. Purity was a theological category as well as a hygienic one. Physical impurity was seen as a sign of moral impurity, so that dirty hands pointed to a dirty heart. Touching a corpse, or a leper, or a pig got you banished from the Lord's table. You had to go through a lengthy process of purification before you could come back again, because for the Pharisees contagion was everywhere—not just physical germs but spiritual ones too. The world was dirty. Sinners were dirty, and all that dirt was dangerous, not only to people's bodies but also to their souls. So purity laws were set up to protect true believers from contagion.

That is why the Pharisees were so appalled when Jesus' disciples dug into their lunch without washing their hands first. It was not just bad manners; it was bad faith. They were ignoring the laws God had set up for their health. They were defying the tradition of the elders, although there is no evidence that they were doing it on purpose. Jesus was an educated Jew; his followers were not. They were his students—former fishermen, day laborers, civil servants—not a Pharisee among them. They had not adopted priestly standards for themselves. Jesus had never encouraged them to.

He was quite careless about the purity laws, as a matter of fact. In the short time they had been with him, they had already watched him lay hands on a leper and a dead child, send a bunch of pigs over a cliff, sit down to supper with a house full of sinners and violate the sabbath without a moment's remorse. He did not seem to care about such things. He harped on other things instead—forgiveness, self-sacrifice, the power of love.

So when the Pharisees criticized his disciples, he lit into them. Stop kicking the dog, he said, and go look in the mirror. You are so careful about how you live and what you eat and the company you keep, but none of that will keep you safe. The danger is not outside of you, waiting to creep into you through your mouth. It is already inside of you, in your own heart. If you want to be pure, start there, with yourself, instead of blaming the dirt on everyone else.

We do not have overt purity laws anymore, so I guess you could call this an outdated story, but we do not seem to have lost our appetite for scapegoats. Last week I saw two movies I have been waiting for—*Philadelphia* and *Schindler's List*. In both of them, certain groups of people are declared unclean—people with AIDS in one, Jews in the other. They are both excluded from the ranks of humanity, shunned by people who consider themselves clean. If they can just get rid of the defective people, the clean people think, then the world will be a safer place for their own children. If they can just avoid contact with them, then they will not get sick themselves.

I will never forget one scene from *Schindler's List*, in which the Nazi commandant Amon Goeth has fallen in love with Helen Hirsch, his Jewish maid. One night he goes down to the cellar where she lives—ostensibly to thank her for her hard work—but before long he is circling her while she stands there speechless, dressed in nothing but her white slip. "I understand that, strictly speaking, you are not a human being," he says to her. "You are a Jewish vermin, I know, but I ask you," he says, reaching out to touch her face and then yanking his hand back as if he has been stung, "are those the eyes of a rodent? Are those the lips of a rodent? Is that the hair of a rodent?"

In his own insane way, he is struggling with his purity law. He is a high-ranking member of a superior race. She is the enemy, the germ that threatens to bring his race down. And yet he loves her. And yet he cannot love her, not without contaminating himself, so he beats her instead, wrecking the cellar and her face at the same time. Who is the rodent here?

It is such an important thing that Jesus knows about us, and it is so hard for us to hear him. The danger is not out there, with the people who frighten and disturb us. The danger is in here, in the part of us that wants to cut ourselves off from them. There is actual evil in the world, no doubt about it, but until we meet up with the evil in ourselves, we cannot do battle. We cannot fight the shadow we will not own.

Mother Teresa knows it. Someone asked her why she does what she does and she replied that she engages in her ministry of love because she knows there is a Hitler inside of her. Does that shock you? It does not shock Jesus. He knows the full potential of our hearts for good and evil. He just wishes we knew it too. Meanwhile, he volunteers himself to everyone who still needs a scapegoat. I will take the blame, he says, you can give it to me. Give me what you hate, what you fear, out there and in here. I am not afraid of getting dirty. Germs don't scare me. Now sit down at my table, whoever you are. Take. Eat. This is my body, given for you.

Nineteen

Sapping God's Strength

Then Jesus said to them, "Prophets are not without honor, except in their hometown, and among their own kin, and in their own house." And he could do no deed of power there, except that he laid his hands on a few sick people and cured them. And he was amazed at their unbelief.

MARK 6:4–6

THE BIBLE IS FULL OF MIRACLE STORIES ABOUT Jesus: how he calmed the storm, how he fed the crowd, how he healed the sick and raised the dead. Those mighty acts got people's attention. They made people take Jesus seriously, even when they could not figure out who he was, exactly, or how they should respond to him. His miracles marked him as someone of real power, only he was operating outside the normal channels of power, and that always causes problems. The channels are there for a reason. They give some people a way of understanding power and gaining access to it. They give other people a way of controlling it. Power that is exercised in certain ways by certain approved personnel is official power. All other exercises of power are suspect, because they challenge the status quo, which has a mandate to defend itself.

Sometimes that is helpful, when the unauthorized power is destructive power—a band of outlaws galloping through town, say, or a guerrilla army fighting its way toward the state capitol. But the same defenses that keep out the bad kind of power may also keep out the good kind, which is what happened to Jesus. He showed up out of nowhere, carrying no one's badge or seal of approval, and he started acting powerful. What he said fit no one's script. What he did fit no one's mold, and so he too became a kind of outlaw—God's own guerrilla—working unauthorized miracles with unapproved people.

Except in the sixth chapter of Mark. In that chapter of his life, Jesus could not do anything but a few simple cures. Why? Because he ran into such a wall of disbelief that it incapacitated him. Or rather it incapacitated *them*, the disbelievers who took offense at him. He did not change. He stayed who he was in their presence. He still had power to share with them, only he could not do anything with it because they would not let him. If you have ever pressed a lit match to a pile of wet sticks, then you know what it was like. It does not matter how strong your flame is; what you need is something that will catch fire.

So call this an "un-miracle" story, in which Jesus held the match until it burned out in his hand, while his family and friends sat shaking their heads a safe distance away. I imagine it stung him, to get his first taste of rejection at home. He had been doing so well before he got there. Simon's mother-in-law was feeling fine, the Gerasene demoniac was back home with his family, and Jairus' daughter was playing jump rope with her friends. Jesus had been preaching and teaching all over Galilee and had collected a small band of followers who were ready to learn from him.

His ministry was off to a strong start, and I expect he was eager to share that with the people who had raised him—not just his mother and brothers and sisters but also the neighbors who had kept him when his mother was sick, and the shopkeepers who had let him run errands for them, and the old men who had leaned on their sticks in the heat of the day and told him stories that made his hair stand on end. He was their son too, so of course he went home to them, wanting to give them the best of what he had to offer.

They welcomed him, apparently, inviting him to speak at synagogue on the sabbath. He was their hometown boy made good, and they wanted to hear what he had learned during his time away. So they all filed in to hear him, smiling and nudging each other before he even got started, each of them taking credit for what a fine young man he had turned out to be. At least until they heard what he had to say. Mark does not tell us what it was, but it was strong enough to astound them at first and then to make them start asking questions. "Is not this the carpenter, the son of Mary . . . ?" That is what they asked each other behind their hands, only it was a hypothetical question.

They knew good and well whose son he was, but by calling him Mary's son they cast doubt on his parentage. In those days, the only reason to identify someone by his mother was because no one knew for sure who his father was, which turns the question into a slur. "Is not this the son of Mary and the brother of James and Joses and Judas and Simon, and are not his sisters here with us?" He was familiar to them. That was the point. They knew him as the eldest child of a large clan, a child like their own children, none of whom was traipsing around the countryside cleansing lepers and casting out demons.

So they took offense at him, and that was that. He dropped the match when it burned his fingers and absolutely nothing caught fire in the synagogue that day. It was his first big failure, the only time in all four of the gospels that Jesus was unable to do something, and the last time in Mark's gospel that he ever appeared in a synagogue on the sabbath. His own people rejected him and he got the message: "Prophets are not without honor, except in their hometown, and among their own kin, and in their own house." He could have rejected them right back, but that was not what he did. He was amazed at their unbelief, that was all, and then he left them to go shine his light somewhere else.

This is a fine story as long as I can keep it at a distance. Like a lot of other stories in the Bible, it is about people who never woke up to Jesus' power and it is easy to judge them from this distance. Dumb Nazarenes. Dumb scribes and Pharisees. The only problem is that they are us. Think about it: the Bible was written by Jews about Jews, which makes it the greatest true confession in the world. It was written by religious people about how their religion tripped them up. It was written by the family about the family member they rejected, although he offered them the best he had to give. Do you have any guesses about who that family is today? It is us, of course. We are the religious people, whose religion can get in our way. We are Jesus' hometown kin, who do not always honor him. The biggest truth this story tells is that the community of faith is one of Jesus' toughest audiences, especially when what he says offends us. We have our own channels of power clearly marked and we are suspicious of people who operate outside of them. We believe we know what is right and what is wrong and we do not welcome anyone who challenges our beliefs.

And yet God is dedicated to doing just that, because it is the only way to get us to believe in God more than we believe in our own beliefs. Jesus was not the only one God sent to shake us up. God is always sending us people to disturb us—to wake us up, to yank our chains, to set us on fire—because about the worst thing that can happen to us, religiously speaking, is for us to hold perfectly still without changing a thing until we turn into fossils. God is not behind us, holding us back. God is ahead of us, calling us forward. God is all around us, speaking to us through the most unlikely people. Sometimes it is a mysterious stranger, but more often, I suspect, it is people so familiar to us that we simply overlook them—our own children and parents, our own friends and neighbors—all of those hometown prophets who challenge us and love us and tell us who we are. The closer they are to us, the less likely we are to hear them, but what a waste of God's resources, to ignore those who know us best.

It is not easy to listen to members of your own family. Our church is a broad church, which means we cover a lot of political and theological territory. Some days I think our differences will kill us, and then I repent. If God is for us, who can be against us? Our differences may in fact bring us life, if only we can manage to unstop our ears and listen to each other. If we cannot, then we should not be surprised if Jesus leaves us to go shine his light somewhere else. Because he cannot make us love each other. He cannot even make us listen to him. All he can do is light his match and wait to see what we will do. Mark's un-miracle story is proof that we can blow it out. We—his own family—are able to sap God's strength by our unwillingness to believe him. We are also able to listen to him and to choose new life.

I believe we have everything—and everyone—we need to hear what God has to say to us. We have God's stories and God's food. We have a baptism that calls us to love and respect each other. And we have each other's stories, which are full of God's graceful power. Let's not let Jesus get away from us again. Let's listen to him, and to each other, and live together like people who believe.

Twenty

A Fixed Chasm

⌐

There was a rich man who was dressed in purple and fine linen
and who feasted sumptuously every day. And at his gate lay
a poor man named Lazarus, covered with sores, who longed
to satisfy his hunger with what fell from the rich man's table;
even the dogs would come and lick his sores.

LUKE 16:19–21

EACH OF US, I BELIEVE, HAS THINGS WE TELL OUR-
selves to protect us from the pain of those around us. If
only he had not dropped out of high school. If only she had not
had so many babies. If he would just learn more English. If she
would only stop drinking. It is human nature to find some reason
why people are the way they are, so that we can get on with the
business of being the way we are without too much drag on our
consciences.

Most of us learned a long time ago that the chief person we
are responsible for is ourselves. We have been put on earth to
love our neighbors, but changing their lot in life is up to them,
not us, especially in a culture like ours that puts so much stock
in individual initiative. The great American myth is that anyone
willing to work hard can win first prize. It might be true if everyone were standing at the same starting line when the gun went
off, but that is never the case. Some start from so far back that

they can run until their lungs burst and never even see the dust of the front runners.

Those are the hardest cases, I think, people who have inherited poverty as surely as they have inherited brown eyes or curly hair, who hear the starting gun go off and do not even know which way to run. Not that it matters. They do not have the right shoes, cannot pay the registration fee, never got a copy of the rules, and are in terrible shape anyway. Other people look at them and think "losers." It has been going on for so long that even people who start much further ahead in the race believe that the difference between themselves and others is so great that it is almost like God had something to do with it. Maybe their misfortune is no mistake. Maybe it is God's punishment for their sins—known or unknown—and by the same token, maybe those who do have more have it because God likes them better. It is even written in the Bible: "For to those who have, more will be given; and from those who do not have, even what they seem to have will be taken away" (Luke 8:18).

This was a popular view in Jesus' day, especially among the rich, who had no trouble finding passages of scripture to back them up. Deuteronomy 28 promises fertility, prosperity, and victory in war to those who obey the Lord. Psalm 1 makes it very clear that the Lord watches over the way of the righteous, but the way of the wicked will perish. Verses like these were used by some first-century religious people to link wealth with God's favor, so that mammon was not a bad thing at all. It was a very good thing, as a matter of fact, a sure sign of God's pleasure.

Those who obeyed God were blessed with material rewards and those who did not were condemned to poverty, which worked out nicely on two counts. It not only allowed the rich to enjoy their riches; it also allowed them to walk past the beggars who slept by their garbage cans without even looking down. Who were they, after all, to interfere with the punishment God had arranged for those poor souls? The best thing was to leave well enough alone. Let the poor pick themselves up and dust themselves off. Let them try harder to do what was right, and God might smile upon them too. Meanwhile, the gap between rich and poor was not anyone's fault. It was God's doing and that, as they say, was that.

It is called "health and wealth theology" and you do not need me to tell you that it is still around. Jesus could not stand it, and what he really hated was that way of reading scripture. There was plenty in Moses and the prophets that went the other way, but those were not the passages that rich people memorized, passages like "Open your hand to the poor and needy neighbor in your land" (Deuteronomy 15:11) or "Those who oppress the poor insult their Maker, but those who are kind to the needy honor him" (Proverbs 14:31). Passages like those made it clear that—far from judging the poor—God identified with them. To walk past a beggar was to walk past God, and woe to the rich person who did.

As usual, Jesus' way of getting his message across was to tell a story. It is an awful story all the way around—the oozing sores, the slobbering dogs, the place of torment, the great chasm. When most of us hear it we plummet right into our own chasm of guilt even though that is not the point. The point of the story is to tell us a truth we need to know in hopes that it will change our lives. Otherwise, God could care less about our guilt. The only thing guilt is good for is to move us to change. If it does not do that, then it is just a sorry substitute for new life. "I can't do what you're asking me, God, but I sure do feel bad about it. Will you settle for that?"

For better or worse, there is very little guilt in this story. As far as I can tell, the rich man does not feel badly about anything except the place where his life of luxury has landed him. He liked the distance between him and Lazarus fine when it was his own doing, but now that the distance seems fixed for good he is in some distress, especially since Lazarus has something he really wants.

Some of you know the Cotton Patch version of this parable, which goes like this: "'Oh, Father Abraham, send me my water boy. Water boy! Quick! I'm just about to perish down here. I need a drink of water.' That old rich guy had always hollered for his water boy: 'Boy, bring me water! Boy, bring me this! Boy, bring me that! Get away, boy! Come here, boy!'"[1]

Even on the far side of the grave the rich man does not recognize the poor man as a fellow human being. He still sees him as something less. He thinks Lazarus is Father Abraham's gofer, someone to fetch water and take messages, but Father Abraham sets him straight. Cradling old bony Lazarus in his bosom, he says no, no, and no. The rich man's days of getting other people to do his bidding are over. Furthermore, there will be no special messages brought back from the dead for his brothers. They have Moses and the prophets just as everyone else does, and if that is not enough to get their attention then no ghost is going to get it either. The end.

I told you it was an awful story. But remember: this story is for us, not against us. Jesus may have enjoyed snatching knots in the tails of his money-loving listeners, but I would be surprised if that were all he wanted. Even when he got angry he got angry for a reason, usually because he could not stand the way people loved the things they could get for themselves better than they loved the things God wanted to give them. They were satisfied with linen suits and sumptuous feasts when God wanted to give them the kingdom. They were content to live in the world with beggars and "boys" when God wanted to give them brothers and sisters. They were happy to get by with the parts of the Bible that backed up their own ways of life when God wanted to give them a new life altogether.

What they did not seem to know—what we still do not seem to know—is that we are the victims of our own way of life. When we succeed in cutting ourselves off from each other, when we learn how to live with the misery of other people by convincing ourselves that they deserve it, when we defend our own good fortune as God's blessing and decline to see how our lives are quilted together with all other lives, then we are the losers. Not because of what God will do to us, but because of what we have done to ourselves. Who do you think fixed that chasm in the story? Was it God or the rich man? Sometimes I think the worst thing we ever have to fear is that God will give us exactly what we want.

The best thing about this story is that it is not over yet. For the rich man, yes, but not for us, because we are the five brothers. Even though Father Abraham would not let Lazarus come back from the grave to tell us this story, Jesus has sneaked it out for us. Now we have that as well as Moses and the prophets *and* someone who has risen from the dead to convince us it is true. All that remains to be seen is what we will do about it.

Note

1. Clarence Jordan and Bill Lane Doulos, *Cotton Patch Parables of Liberation* (Scottdale, Penn.: Herald Press, 1976), 67.

Twenty-One

Shock Therapy

If your hand causes you to stumble, cut it off; it is better for you to enter life maimed than to have two hands and to go to hell, to the unquenchable fire.

MARK 9:43

WHEN I WAS A CHAPLAIN AT GEORGIA BAPTIST Medical Center in Atlanta, one of the requirements of the job was taking part in periodic disaster drills. The whole hospital was divided up into blue, green, red, and yellow areas where hospital staff were instructed to go in teams when we heard the siren blow. Red for triage, blue for surgery, green for treatment and release. I will never forget the time I got assigned to yellow: the morgue. When the siren blew, I climbed the stairs to the top floor where no one ever went and met the strange little man in charge of the cold storage room.

While we waited for the drill to end, he offered to show me around. I was trying to think of a polite way to say "Not on your life" when he opened a large freezer—the big rectangular kind that sits on the floor and opens like a trunk. "This is where we keep the frozen specimens," he said, and before I could turn away I got a glimpse of the amputated limbs inside. I will spare you the details, but it was enough to wreck my sleep for weeks.

It was nightmare material, just like this passage from Mark's gospel. Nowhere in all the New Testament is Jesus so graphic about the wages of sin. Better you should hang a rock around your neck and jump into the ocean, he says, better you should maim and blind yourself than walk around like nothing is wrong until the disaster siren sounds and you find yourself assigned to hell, where the worm never dies and the fire is never quenched.

This does not show up on many people's lists of favorite Bible passages. It is too primitive, too grotesque, and it seems to commend self-mutilation, which does not sound like Jesus at all. The one thing I like about it, though, is that it defines the limits of literalism. Walk into the most Bible-believing church you can find—where the women do not wear trousers or speak in church, where the men do not swear oaths or mow their lawns on Sundays—go into a place as strict as that and I bet you won't find many people with eye patches and wrapped stumps, because even the most literal Christians balk at this passage. It goes against their reason, not to mention their sense of self-preservation. They become biblical critics just like the rest of us, which does not mean we *criticize* the Bible but that we ask important questions of it. Whom is Jesus talking to in this passage and what is his purpose? Is he speaking literally or figuratively? Has Mark taken liberties in writing things down?

Chronologically speaking, these are Jesus' last words in his homeland. When he is finished he will travel south from Galilee into Judea, where death awaits him in Jerusalem. This speech before he goes is part of his instructions to his disciples—the leadership seminar he began several verses before with the little child on his lap. He is telling them what is good for them. "*It would be better for you . . .*" he says four times, describing several awful things that would be better for them than to cause a little one to stumble or to stumble themselves. Better they should cripple

themselves than do that, he warns them. Better they should limp
and grope their way into the kingdom of God than be thrown
whole and healthy into hell.

So one thing Jesus is trying to do is to impress upon them the
importance of their actions. Following him is no casual thing.
It is a life-or-death decision that is about to get very dangerous
for everyone involved—not only because of what other people
may do to them, but because of what they may do to themselves
by failing to take themselves seriously enough. As disciples, they
have no time off. They cannot take a break and go tell Polack
jokes or harass a pretty girl to make her blush. They cannot let
off a little steam by turning over tables at the local pub or ganging
up on religious rivals to put them out of business.

Everything they do has consequences. Everything they say
counts. They are either part of the good news or they are simply
bad news, but they are neither invisible nor insignificant. Their
lives matter. Their words matter. They have power they do not
even know about, and if they use it to cause someone to stumble—
to lose faith, to question God, to pull away from the light—then
they would be better off at the bottom of the sea.

That makes this passage a threat, but also a promise. The
disciples are full of unrealized power, and Jesus is begging them
to wake up to it and use it wisely. He is also reminding them
that there is a spiritual reality much more solid than the physical
reality they are so careful about.

One of the reasons we recoil from this passage, I think, is that
it attacks our physical reality. Cut off our precious hands and feet?
Gouge out our lovely eyes? Our very horror shows us how much
we value our wholeness, our ability to see and touch and walk on
our own two feet. Fine, Jesus says. Do not take me literally, but
take me seriously: you have a soul that is just as precious and
lovely as your body, and its wholeness comes first. If it is sick,

you are sick all over and if it is crippled then your two good legs cannot take you anywhere worth going.

Why doesn't *that* make us flinch, I wonder? Why aren't we as careful of our souls as we are of our bodies? At the very least, these scary words of Jesus are shock therapy, designed to get our attention and keep it. What we do matters. What we say counts. We have power we do not even know about, and it is absolutely crucial that we use it to build up and not to tear down.

I have spent a lot of time thinking about stumbling: how we do it, how we cause others to do it. Talking one way and acting another. Talking about how we are all God's children and then treating some of those children like stepchildren or worse yet like orphans, putting them away somewhere and then forgetting to visit. Talking about God's good gifts to us and then hoarding those gifts like misers, refusing to share ourselves, refusing to share what we have with others. Talking about God's amazing grace and then saving up our own old hurts like green stamps in a book—the time he did this, the time she said that—a catalog of griefs that collects bitterness like dust.

People who know us notice these things. They trip over them, just like we do, and some people will even tell you it is why they have lost interest in church. They cannot see any difference between the people inside the church and the people outside the church, except that the people outside do not pretend to be any better than they are. On the one hand I think, "Of course. The church is for sinners, not Pharisees." On the other hand I think, "That's no excuse."

If there is anyone in the world equipped to care for people body and soul, we are. We are God's baptized, who have been given the gift of second sight. We can see spirit as well as flesh. We know there is more going on than meets the eye. When we look at people, we see them whole, the way God meant them to be. When they are not whole, it hurts us, as if we are missing something we need for ourselves. Because of this, disciples cannot take part in anything that diminishes the soul of another human being. Disciples cannot stand by while anyone is called names, or talked down to, or cast out, because all those things wound the soul, perhaps even murder it, and it would be better for us to chop off pieces of our own bodies than to let that happen to us or to anyone else.

I do not believe God has a cold storage room like the morgue at Georgia Baptist Medical Center. I believe God's will for us is abundant life. I do believe that we can put ourselves into cold storage any day of our lives by failing to live up to the love that is in us. A wasted existence is hell, no two ways about it. Fortunately, there is an alternative. If we want to be whole, we can use our two good eyes to see the world the way God sees it and we can use our two good feet to carry us into it as deeply as we dare, and we can stretch out our still-attached arms to someone in danger of stumbling, so that God can steady and save us all.

Twenty-two

Why Did You Doubt?

—

Peter answered him, "Lord, if it is you, command me to come to you on the water." He said, "Come." So Peter got out of the boat, started walking on the water, and came toward Jesus.

MATTHEW 14:28–29

THERE IS A STORY FROM THE ZEN BUDDHIST TRADI-
tion about the disciple who thought he could improve his
chances of enlightenment by seeking it on his own, so he bid
farewell to his brothers in the monastery, took the ferry across
the river, and went to live in a cave high in the hills all by himself.
There he meditated nonstop for twenty-five years. At the end of
that time, he emerged from the cave, stretched his arms above
his head like a man waking from a long sleep, and made his way
down to the river.

Without even pausing to test the temperature first, he stepped
out on the water and proceeded to walk across it toward the monastery he had left a quarter of a century ago. Two monks who were
doing their laundry that morning saw him coming across the river.

"Who is that?" one of them asked. The other replied, "That is
the old man who has spent twenty-five years meditating in a cave.
Now look at him! He can walk on water!"

"What a pity," the first monk said. "The ferry only costs a
quarter."

The Christian tradition has its own water-walking stories, the most famous of which is Peter's attempt to meet Jesus on the stormy sea of Galilee. He did not prepare for twenty-five years to do it. He did not practice at all, as far as anyone knows. He simply saw Jesus out on the water and asked his Lord to command him to come—not to allow him, but to make him—so that Peter would have no further doubt about who Jesus was.

For most of the years of its telling, this story has been repeated as a story about faith. Peter, in the end, does not have enough. He steps out on the water like an Olympic hopeful on the balance beam, laying each foot down on the water without a tremor. Then the wind gusts, he loses focus and down he goes, while everyone in the boat watches helplessly.

If Peter had just kept his eyes on Jesus. If he had just had *more faith*, then his fear might not have sunk him. That is how I have always heard the story told, but I wonder, because there is a peculiar thing Peter says at the beginning of the story that makes me doubt his motives. Once Jesus has appeared on the sea, walking toward the disciples, and has assured them that it is he, Peter says, "Lord, if it is you, command me to come to you on the water." He doubts Jesus, in other words. He doubts Jesus is who he says he is and demands proof of his identity, using the very same phrase the devil used when he tempted Jesus in the wilderness: "*If* you are the son of God. . . ." Do this thing, then this, then this.

It is not enough for Peter that Jesus is headed straight for the boat. Peter stops him before he gets there, putting himself out front as a kind of dare. "Lord, if it is you, command me to come to you on the water." Make me do something extraordinary. Set me apart from these other men. Grant me an exemption from the laws that bind ordinary people and I will believe that you are who you say you are.

It is incredibly pompous of Peter, but in this story, as in most of the other embarrassing stories about Peter, he is speaking for us. Is there anyone among us who has never asked God for an exemption? Please, God, suspend the rules just this once and make me know that you are there. Heal me, help me, talk to me out loud. Leave me no room to doubt you and I will believe.

We have all got a little bit of the devil in us, asking Jesus to prove himself by doing something spectacular for us. We want the burden of proof to be on him, not us. We want him to single us out for special treatment, to let us climb out of the boat and do a solo no one else gets to do—and maybe even get extra credit for volunteering to do it (look at him, so brave, so faithful, such a spiritual warrior).

I expect Jesus had to think a minute before he decided how to respond to Peter. He could have said, "Who do you think you are, Simon Peter? Sit back down and find your oar!" But that was not what Peter needed. What Peter needed was a couple of steps on the water (to cure his doubt) and then a nose full of sea water (to cure his pomposity).

"Lord, save me!" he cried when he began to sink, which is how we know he got his question answered in the end. He was not in any doubt who Jesus was when the sea gave way beneath him. He knew both who Jesus was and what he was for: he was the Lord, the life saver. Jesus did not let him down, either. He reached out his hand, caught Peter, and threw him in the boat like a big fish, saying, "You of little faith, why did you doubt?"

That stinging rebuke is usually heard as Jesus' judgment on Peter's sinking, but I think it might just as easily be a comment on Peter's grandstanding in the first place: "Lord, if it is you, command me to come to you on the water." That was when Peter's doubt flared up. What happened later on the water was simply an extension of it, as he tried to make Jesus put an end to his uncertainty.

"You of little faith, why did you doubt?" Jesus said to him afterwards. I was headed straight for you. I told you who I was. If you had kept your seat for one minute more I would have been sitting right next to you, you and all the others, with no need for that circus stunt out on the water. (The ferry only costs a quarter.)

He only says that to Peter, by the way. There is no rebuke for the others, who had faith enough to stay in the boat, hauling on the oars together until their Lord came to them. Only Peter left the boat and the community in order to do a solo—thinking, perhaps, that it would go down in history as a sign of great faith—never guessing that Jesus would call it the exact opposite.

You decide. Maybe this really is a story about the church's need for heroes—for people who, like Peter, are willing to risk their lives to prove that Jesus is who he says he is. But it may just as well be a story about the other eleven disciples, who never thought of themselves as particularly heroic, who never dreamed of putting Jesus to the test, who were willing to row against the wind until he got into the boat with them, no matter how long it took.

They were not looking for exemptions. They were just looking for their Lord to join them where they were, and that was when the miracle happened—not while he and Peter were out doing the fancy stuff on the water, but once he had everyone back together in the boat.

That was when the wind ceased—shhh—just like that. And those in the boat worshiped him saying, "Truly, you are the Son of God."

Twenty-three

Chickens and Foxes

At that very hour some Pharisees came and said to him, "Get away from here, for Herod wants to kill you." Jesus said to them, "Go and tell that fox for me, 'Listen, I am casting out demons and performing cures today and tomorrow, and on the third day I finish my work.'"

LUKE 13:31–32

MORE AND MORE I AM CONVINCED THAT WE MISS something vital to our faith when we insist on approaching God one by one. Our individual relationships with God are very important, but they do not make us the body of Christ. It is our life together that makes us Christ's body, a mysterious organism that is much more than a collection of individuals. When we come together to worship, we form a new being with a name and an address, which has its own life and reputation. We call it the church—not the building but the people—a phenomenon that has been around longer than any of us. When you or I identify ourselves as members of the church, we get credit for things we did not do.

We may also get blame for things we did not do, but the point is, the church is more than its individual members. We have a community identity and a community mandate. We stand for something, which it behooves us to recall from time to time. Do

we, as a body, resemble Christ or have we taken on the character-
istics of someone else? Are we true to our head or are we giving
him a headache by yanking away and refusing to belong to him?

In the thirteenth chapter of Luke you can hear the kind of anguish we cause Jesus when we do that. "Jerusalem, Jerusalem, the
city that kills the prophets and stones those who are sent to it!" he
says, choked with tears. "How often have I desired to gather your
children together as a hen gathers her brood under her wings,
and you were not willing!" It is the lament of one whose love has
been scorned, whose protection has been rejected.

At risk of his own life, Jesus has brought the precious kingdom of God within the reach of the beloved city of God, but
the city of God is not interested. Jerusalem has better things to
do than to hide under the shelter of this mother hen's wings. It
has a fox as its head, who commands a great deal more respect.
Consider the contrast: Jesus has disciples; Herod has soldiers.
Jesus serves; Herod rules. Jesus prays for his enemies; Herod
kills his. In a contest between a fox and a chicken, whom would
you bet on?

Several years ago I visited the Holy Land, and one of the places
I remember best is the small chapel on a hill opposite Jerusalem,
built on the spot where tradition holds that Jesus wept for the
city. I remember it because the wall behind the altar was made out
of glass, giving visitors a splendid view of the skyline of Jerusalem.
I also remember it because there was the image of a rooster on
the front of the altar—a bright, fierce-looking bird made out of
colored tiles with a flock of little chicks under his wings.

A *rooster?* That's what I thought when I saw it. Jesus did not
say "rooster." Jesus said "hen," but I think I know why the artist
took liberties with the text. A rooster can defend himself. He has
sharp spikes on the back of his feet that work like little stilettos
on anyone who bothers him. A rooster can also peck pretty hard,

and he does not wait for you to peck first. If you have ever tried to get eggs from a hen house with a rooster on the loose, then you know what I mean.

And yet Jesus did not liken himself to a rooster. He likened himself to a brooding hen, whose chief purpose in life is to protect her young, with nothing much in the way of a beak and nothing at all in the way of talons. About all she can do is fluff herself up and sit on her chicks. She can also put herself between them and the fox, as ill-equipped as she is. At the very least, she can hope that she satisfies his appetite so that he leaves her babies alone.

How do you like that image of God? If you are like me, it is fine in terms of comfort, but in terms of protection it leaves something to be desired. When the foxes of this world start prowling really close to home, when you can hear them snuffling right outside the door, then it would be nice to have a little bigger defense budget for the hen house.

Maybe some of you saw the Clint Eastwood movie called *Pale Rider* that came out several years ago. Clergy in the Atlanta area were sent invitations to a special preview, so I went, wondering what in the world this movie had to do with the church. As it turned out, Clint played a frontier preacher with a past. What kind of past was never clear, but he walked around in a clerical collar looking deeply pained, and once when he took his shirt off you could see the scars of three old bullet holes in his back.

One day he rode into a mining town that had been overrun by foxes. The corrupt sheriff was in cahoots with a bunch of armed bullies who were always taking things that did not belong to them and then killing anyone who got in their way. At first Clint just took it all in, getting clear who the foxes were and where their lair was.

Then one day he calmly walked into the bank and produced the key to a safe deposit box (a clue to his past, in that very town!).

Alone in the vault, he pulled the box from the wall and opened the lid. Inside was a pair of six shooters and a belt full of bullets. Clint carefully took it out and strapped it around his waist. Then he took off his clerical collar and put it in the box while all the clergy in the audience went wild. Yes!! Go get 'em, Clint!! Gun down those foxes and nail their tails to the wall!! Which is exactly what he did, to the great satisfaction of everyone in the theater, including me.

That was Clint Eastwood, but Jesus was Jesus. He too bore old scars on his body. He too meant to protect the chicks from the foxes but he would not become a fox himself in order to do it. He refused to fight fire with fire. When Herod and his bullies came after Jesus and his brood, he did not produce any six shooters to stop them in their tracks. He just put himself between them and the chicks, all fluffed up and hunkered down like a mother hen.

It may have looked like a minor skirmish to those who were there, but that contest between the chicken and the fox turned out to be the cosmic battle of all time, in which the power of tooth and fang was put up against the power of a mother's love for her chicks. And God bet the farm on the hen.

Depending on whom you believe, she won. It did not look that way at first, with feathers all over the place and chicks running for cover. But as time went on, it became clear what she had done. She had refused to run from the foxes, and she had refused to become one of them. Having loved her own who were in the world, she loved them to the end. She died a mother hen, and afterwards she came back to them with teeth marks on her body to make sure they got the point: that the power of foxes could not kill her love for them, nor could it steal them away from her. They might have to go through what she went through in order to get past the foxes, but she would be waiting for them on the other side, with love stronger than death.

I have never really thought about the church as a mother hen, but I am thinking about it now. The church of Christ as a big fluffed up brooding hen, offering warmth and shelter to all kinds of chicks, including orphans, runts, and maybe even a couple of ducks. The church of Christ planting herself between the foxes of this world and the fragile-boned chicks, offering herself up to be eaten before she will sacrifice one of her brood. The church of Christ staying true to whose body she is, by refusing to run from the foxes and refusing to become one of them.

Who would have thought being a mother hen offered such opportunities for courage? Maybe that is why the church is called "Mother Church." It is where we come to be fed and sheltered, but it is also where we come to stand firm with those who need the same things from us. It is where we grow from chicks into chickens, by giving what we have received, by teaching what we have learned, and by loving the way we ourselves have been loved—by a mother hen who would give his life to gather us under his wings.

Apocalyptic Figs

Twenty-Four

Last of All

⌐

Jesus sat down, called the twelve, and said to them, "Whoever
wants to be first must be last of all and servant of all." Then he
took a little child and put it among them; and taking it in his
arms, he said to them, "Whoever welcomes one such child in my
name welcomes me, and whoever welcomes me welcomes not me
but the one who sent me."

MARK 9:35–37

JESUS HAD A THING ABOUT CHILDREN. WHILE OTHER
people tended to ignore anyone shorter than their own knee-
caps, Jesus saw what was going on down there. He saw the toddlers hanging onto their mothers' skirts and shrinking away
from the stray dogs, the wagon wheels, and the donkey dung
that no one up top seemed aware of. He saw them trying to keep
up with the grown-ups when they walked—gamely at first and
then quickly defeated, limping along with one arm pulled half
out of its socket by tall people with giant strides. He saw how
the adults coo-cooed to them when there was nothing else going
on but quickly lost interest in them the moment another adult
appeared.

Children were fillers, not main events. They were gifts of God
who would be useful someday—to look after their parents, to
hold down responsible jobs, to have children of their own—but

meanwhile they were non-entities—fuzzy caterpillars to be fed and sheltered until they could turn into butterflies.

Jesus seemed to like them just the way they were, which was unusual for a man, and especially for a bachelor. Although he had none of his own, Jesus was not afraid of babies. He took them in his arms and blessed them. He knew how to put his hand behind their wobbly heads, how to pass them back to their mothers without dropping them. Even the two-year-olds did not bother him. He never asked their parents please to take them to the nursery. On the contrary, when his disciples scolded people for bringing their children to church, Jesus was indignant. The kingdom belongs to such as these, he said. They are full-fledged citizens of God's realm—not later but right now.

This partiality may not sound as strange now as it did back then, because we are much more tuned into children than first-century Palestinians ever were. Far from ignoring children, middle-class Americans tend to idealize them, dressing them in Ralph Lauren fashions, putting them in first-grade French classes and setting a place for them at adult dinner parties. Maybe we lavish the attention on them we wish someone had lavished on us, but in any case children are much more visible (and audible) in the adult world than they have ever been before.

Maybe you read the article in the paper about Lisa Brown, the Houston attorney who brought her five-month-old daughter to a deposition and drove her opposing counsel crazy. He retaliated by filing a motion to "exclude gurgling infant" from future depositions. "The child's presence is a distraction and unprofessional," his motion states, "precisely because the baby behaves normally for a baby."

He lost, but his objection lets me know that there are limits to our tolerance of children. Yes, they are innocent, playful, vulnerable, honest, fresh-faced, and loving, especially if you are only around them for about fifteen minutes a day. But if you spend more time with them than that, then you know that children are also noisy, clinging, destructive, self-centered, and surprisingly cruel. The best of them will pluck the whiskers right off a cat if you do not keep an eye on them, or knock other children down for trying to play with their toys. "I love children," wrote Nancy Mitford, "especially when they cry, for then someone will take them away."

So I do not think Jesus was holding them up as moral examples when he took children in his arms and blessed them. He did not say we should imitate them, after all. He just said that when we welcome them in his name we welcome him, and that when we welcome him we welcome God. That is a pretty amazing equation, if you think about it.

Do you want to spend some time with God? Then get down on the floor with little Sarah over there. Get fingerpaint all over your clothes and laugh at her dumb jokes and never mind that you have more important things to do, like finishing the laundry or earning a living. She is not filler. She is the main event. Opening yourself up to her is better for your soul than finishing a project or getting a raise or even reading a whole book of the Bible.

There will be no payback. Oh, she may shout your name next time she sees you and run to hug your knees, but you cannot list her as a job reference or ask her to lend you a hundred dollars to get your car fixed. She is not good for anything like that. She is not in charge of anything, she cannot buy you anything, she will not even remember your birthday or invite you over for supper with some friends. She has no status, no influence, no income, which makes her great in God's eyes. She is just what you need. And you, you are able to work on your own greatness by understanding that it is what you do when you think no one is looking, with someone who does not count, for no reward, that ushers you into the presence of God.

Do you see what Jesus is up to here? It is one more of his lessons in the topsy-turvy kingdom of God, where the first shall be last and the last shall be first and everyone who thinks he or she is on the top of the heap is in for a big surprise. He is not just talking about children, either. He is talking about all the little ones in this world with no status, no influence, no income. He is daring us to welcome them as bearers of God, to believe that God's hierarchy is the reverse of ours and that greatness is only available to those with no ambition to be great.

The whole lesson came about because he caught the disciples playing "Who's Greatest" on the road to Capernaum. If you were ever caught passing a note in elementary school, then you know how they felt. "What were you arguing about on the way?" he asked them and no one said a word, because they had been fighting about who was the best, the most faithful, the most-likely-to-succeed disciple. Peter, James, and John were the favorites— the first three disciples Jesus called—who still got to go places with him that the others did not. Among them, Peter figured he had it all sewed up because he was the first to call Jesus the Messiah, but the others reminded him that he was also the one whom Jesus called Satan, for refusing to accept Jesus' forecast of his death.

That was the heart of the problem, really. They were arguing about who was greatest because they could not stand what Jesus had said about being killed. They did not understand and they were afraid to ask, so they got as far away from it as they could by playing status games instead. Who is first, who is best, who is greatest. You know what that is like. When you are scared of something, don't ask. Act like there is nothing wrong. Change the subject and talk about something else instead, something that makes you feel big and strong. That is what the disciples were doing, which was why Jesus had to sit them down and give them a leadership seminar right then and there. "Whoever wants to be first must be last of all and servant of all," he told them. Then he showed them what he meant by taking a little child in his arms. They wanted to know who was greatest, so he showed them: twenty-six inches tall, limited vocabulary, unemployed, zero net worth, nobody. God's agent. The last, the least of all.

Our hierarchies are so subtle that half the time we are not even aware of them. One Sunday I was standing outside on the porch of the church after the eleven o'clock service when a man with a sobbing child on his shoulder came out right behind his wife, who held a beaming child by the hand. "What's the matter?" I asked her and she explained. Their eldest son—the beaming one—had just entered third grade and was going to be an aco- lyte. Inside, the deacon and the verger had been showing him the ropes—how to light the candles, how to carry the torches—when his little brother had announced with stars in his eyes that he would like to be an acolyte too. For the umpteenth time in his short life, he was told no, that he was too young, too small, that he would have to wait, and it simply undid him. He was never first, his mother explained. He was always last, and I thought, "God help us, we're doing it right here—making sure the first go first and the last stay last."

I do not know what the answer is. I do not know how you operate a church or a business or a society by turning it over to those with the least to offer, but I do know that God's values are not our values, and that knowledge alone may be enough to keep us humble. However we choose to organize our lives, we have this little child to remind us that God organizes things otherwise, and that if we want to welcome God into our lives then there is no one whom we may safely ignore. In the topsy-turvy kingdom of God, the most unlikely people are most likely to be agents of God—the ones who live in the world below our kneecaps, the ones who are stuck at the end of the line, the ones who are sobbing on someone's shoulder because they are always, always last.

In God's world, things are different. Gurgling babies derail taped depositions. Children run the United Nations. Toddlers are bishops and second sons get to go first, while servants sit down at tables they used to polish and the greatest disciple is the one who waits on them, the one whose name you can never remember (was that Thaddeus or Bartholomew?). If you want to enter this kingdom, there is a way: go find a nobody to put your arms around and say hello to God.

Twenty-five

The Problem with Miracles

~~

Then one of the leaders of the synagogue named Jairus came and, when he saw him, fell at his feet and begged him repeatedly, "My little daughter is at the point of death. Come and lay your hands on her, so that she may be made well, and live."

MARK 5:22–23

SOMETIMES I WONDER IF THE MIRACLE STORIES IN the Bible do more harm than good. They are spectacular stories, most of them, and there is a lot of comfort to be had from watching Jesus still the storm, heal the sick, and raise the dead. His miracles remind us that the way things are is not the way they will always be, and that there is great power available to us through our kinship with him. He is living proof that God's will for us is not chaos but wholeness, and every miracle proclaims that truth. Every healing, every revival, every banishment of evil is like a hole poked in the opaque fabric of time and space. The kingdom breaks through and for a moment or two we see how things will be—or how they really are right now in the mind of God—and then it is over. The disciples go back to their rowing, the once-blind beggar walks off to look for work, the little girl stretches her arms above her head and takes the bread her stunned mother holds out to her.

The problem with miracles is that it is hard to witness them

without wanting one of your own. Every one of us knows someone who is suffering. Every one of us knows someone who could
use a miracle, but miracles are hard to come by. Not everyone who
prays for one gets one, not by a long shot, and meanwhile there
are people who get them without asking for them at all. On the
whole, religious people cannot stand this apparent randomness,
so we spend a lot of time trying to figure out the formula. Surely
there is a formula! Two parts prayer, three parts faith, one part
good works. We comb the miracle stories to find out who did
what right and who did what wrong so that we can learn from
their experience. We imitate their virtues and avoid their faults
in hopes of becoming irresistible to God.

Only most of the time that is hard to do, because God rarely
does anything the same way twice. For instance, in the fifth chapter of Mark's gospel, we get two miracle stories layered together.
First, the story of Jairus and his daughter—one of three resurrection stories in the gospels, not counting Christ's own. It is
the bread of a larger sandwich Mark has prepared for us. The
inside of the sandwich is the story of the woman who has bled
for twelve years, before she touches the hem of Jesus' garment
and is healed.

Mark inserted that second story inside the first one for a
reason, because bleeding women and dead little girls were both
taboo in Judaism. By having anything to do with either one of
them, Jesus rendered himself unclean. That was no sin in itself,
since people could not have babies, care for the sick, or bury the
dead without becoming unclean, only Jesus was not a midwife or
a nurse. He was a holy man, who was expected to steer clear of
defilement. If it happened to him by mistake, as it did the moment the bleeding woman touched him, then according to the law
he should have gone off to purify himself. Until he did, he was
contagious and unfit for holy duty.

But Jesus did not go off to purify himself. He simply sent the healed woman on her way and turned around to follow Jairus again—causing quite a scandal, I imagine, when he stepped inside the man's house. Jairus was a leader of the synagogue, remember, a respected elder in the community whose obedience to the law was a matter of record. For someone like him to seek help from someone like Jesus must have caused a whole lot of talk. It would be like one of us driving right past the medical center to go see a root doctor way out in the country who held tent revivals on the weekends.

So this is not just a story about Jesus or even about the little girl he raised from the dead. It is also a story about Jairus, who broke every rule he knew in order to save his daughter's life. Can you imagine what it must have been like for him, to fall at Jesus' feet in front of a big crowd? And then to lead him through that crowd, only to be stopped short by the woman with the hemorrhage—whose condition was not life-threatening, after all, while his own child's life seeped away—and then to be told that it was too late, that the child was dead and there was no reason to trouble Jesus any further.

This is as bad as it gets. You beg on your knees for help and it comes too late. You give up all your cherished beliefs in order to grab at one last wild straw and it comes off in your hand. The ground rushes up to meet you and just before the sun goes out for good you hear a voice: "Do not fear; only believe." It sounds like a formula, doesn't it? If you will just believe hard enough, your prayers will be answered. If you just have enough faith, things will turn out all right. That is how it worked for Jairus, anyhow. His daughter was saved. The kingdom broke through right there in her bedroom and all the angels sang "Amen," but it simply does not happen that way every time.

Most people do not get a miracle like that, and one of the

meanest things religious people do is to blame it on a lack of faith. I remember when I was a chaplain on the cancer ward at Georgia Baptist Hospital and we finally had to start frisking visitors at the door. A couple of patients had complained that perfect strangers were coming into their rooms, holding hands around their beds and praying for an increase in their clearly inadequate faith. It turned out that a local church was doing this—uninvited—as a part of their healing ministry, only it did not have a healing effect. It had a bludgeoning effect, as people who were already sick got a strong dose of guilt and shame to go along with their chemotherapy.

I believe that the church people were well-intentioned. I also believe they had gotten mixed up about what causes miracles. They thought faith made miracles happen. They thought miracles worked along the same lines as those strength tests you used to see at county fairs, the ones that looked like big thermometers with red ringers at the top. It was all a matter of how hard you could hit the thing with the sledgehammer. If you were really strong, you could ring the bell and win the prize. And if you were not, well, try, try again and better luck next time.

In other words, they thought miracles were something they could control. If you are sick and getting sicker, it must be your own fault. You must try harder. Pump up your faith and ring the bell. Impress God with the power of your belief and claim your miracle as a reward. Only this is idolatry, do you see? This is one more of our pitiful efforts to work things around so that we seem to be in charge of our lives, instead of owning up to the truth that every single breath we take is a free surprise from God. Faith does not work miracles. God does. To concentrate on the strength of our own belief is to practice magic. To concentrate on the strength of God is to practice faith. This is not just semantics. This is the difference between believing our lives are in our own hands and believing they are in God's. God, not faith, works miracles.

Did Jairus' daughter have faith? I do not think so. She was on her way out of the world. Did Jairus have faith? Mark never said so. Jairus just followed Jesus home and watched that unclean holy man do his work. Either way, the high point was not then but earlier, when Jesus told him, "Do not fear, only believe." If Jairus was able to do that, then he would have survived whatever happened next, even if Jesus had walked into his daughter's room, closed her eyes with his fingertips, and pulled the sheet over her head. Her father's belief would have become the miracle at that point, his willingness to believe that she was still in God's good hands even though she had slipped out of his.

It helps me to remember that Jesus prayed for a miracle on the night before he died. "For you all things are possible," he prayed to his abba. "Remove this cup from me." Only when he opened his eyes the cup was still there. Did he lack faith? I do not think so. The miracle was that he drank the cup, believing in the power of God more than he believed in his own. It is always a miracle, isn't it, when we understand that God is God and we are not?

I do not expect any of us will stop praying for miracles. I hope not, because the world needs all the miracles it can get. Every time you hear about one, remember that you are getting a preview of the kingdom. There is simply no formula for success, which is a real relief for those of us who cannot seem to ring the bell. Maybe we cannot do it because it is not our job. "Do not fear; only believe." That is our job. The rest is up to God.

Twenty-six

The Narrow Door

—

*Jesus went through one town and village after another, teaching
as he made his way to Jerusalem. Someone asked him, "Lord,
will only a few be saved?" He said to them, "Strive to enter
through the narrow door; for many, I tell you, will try to enter
and will not be able."*

LUKE 13:22–24

NOT TOO LONG AGO I WAS TALKING TO SOMEONE
from Atlanta who had driven through Clarkesville on his
way to Highlands and had stopped to see Grace-Calvary Church.
"It was late and the office was closed," he said, "so I stood on
tiptoe and looked through the windows. I couldn't see much but
it sure was beautiful. Next time I'll call ahead so you can show
me the inside."

"Did you try the door?" I asked him.

"No," he said. "I just assumed it was locked."

"It's never locked," I said. "We lost the key about a hundred
years ago. You can go inside whenever you want."

He could not believe it, and small wonder. In this day and
age it does not make any sense to leave a church wide open but
we do, and it is one of the things I like best about Grace-Calvary.
When I was welcomed into the life of the congregation, we had
to change the service in the prayer book. Why? Because it said

the senior warden was supposed to give me the key to the church and there was no key. So he gave me a doorstop instead, with a little brass plaque on it that says, "Let the doors of this place be open to all people."

That same phrase appears in the church's mission statement, which begins, "Grace-Calvary's historic doors are open to all people for communion with God and one another in Christ." Even when they are closed to keep the air conditioning in or the cat out, our doors are still open. All it takes is a little tug and anyone can walk in here, day or night, to say hello to God.

I love it, but according to the thirteenth chapter of Luke, the doors to the kingdom are not like this. There is only one door, which is narrow and can most certainly be locked. No one wanders through it by accident. No one comes in for a casual look around. Getting through it is so hard that many will try and fail, Jesus says. They will find they are not strong enough, and after it has been locked they will knock until their knuckles are raw.

They can shout through the door all they want. They can remind the Lord standing behind it that they ate supper with him (doesn't he remember?), that they heard him teaching in their streets, but none of that information will open the door for them. It is not enough that they know what he looks like. It is not enough that they can quote some things he said, because the sad fact is that their lives bear no evidence of relationship with him. They may know him but he does not know them. The acquaintance was too slight to register in his memory, and he tells them to go away.

This is not the Lord most of us are looking for. We are counting on the "Come unto me all ye that labor and are heavy laden" Lord, the one who takes little children in his lap and prefers the company of sinners. We are counting on him to hold the door open for us, to wedge his own body in it if necessary so that we can squeeze through, only that is not who Luke gives us this time.

Instead, he gives us the Lord who knows from his own painful experience that life comes with limits.

Jesus was on his way to Jerusalem, Luke tells us, and you know what that means. Time is limited. Choices are limited. Shallow acquaintance with God will not do. There is no time for it. Those who want to follow Jesus through the door cannot afford to stand way back in the crowd and listen to him teach. It is time for them to elbow their way to the front and present themselves to him. "Here I am. I want you to know me. Put me to work."

So this is at least partly a lesson about limits, I think. As much as we chafe against them, they are great motivators. I remember a professor of mine who used to lock the door when class started. If you were late, you were out of luck. It only took about a week for all of us to become very, very punctual. And I will tell you, it made a real difference in the class. When he came in, we were all ready to begin. There was no drain on our energy like there is when latecomers come dribbling in one after the other, each of them trying to be unobtrusive although they might as well be riding elephants. There was none of that, and while some members of the class accused our teacher of being rigid, the overall effect was one of great mutual regard. He took us seriously and we returned the favor. We found out what we could do when we tried, and he never expected less of us.

Which is fine as far as it goes, but I want to take it a step further because I do not think this passage is simply about trying hard and being on time. You have to remember whom Jesus was talking to. He was on his way to Jerusalem and he was talking to people who were sure God's door would always be open to them. They knew the rules and they played by them. They were not sinners and they were not tax collectors and they fully expected reserved seats in the kingdom, a special section set aside for chosen people living in the promised land.

When Jesus told them no, that they would have to struggle like everyone else and that many of them would not make it, it was like a door slammed shut in their faces. That was one of the reasons they killed him—because he took their security away. He undermined their faith in themselves by suggesting that God's ideas about goodness and badness were different from theirs, so different that people they thought were beneath them might well get into the kingdom ahead of them, and that scared them. If Jesus was right, then they were wrong about a lot of things, but all in all it was easier to get rid of him than it was to change their whole way of life, so that is what they did. They let their fear turn to anger and Jesus was a goner.

All kinds of people say this is a passage about the Jews, but please do not make that mistake. It is about any and all of us who are sure we know the mind of God, who are sure we are on God's side and are sure what God's priorities are. It is about any and all of us who calculate our chances of getting into the kingdom by focusing on the sins of other people, as if we could free up more seats for ourselves by eliminating the competition.

That is not how it works, Jesus says. We cannot assume the door is open any more than we can assume it is closed. There is nothing automatic about it, because the kingdom belongs to God and no amount of human conniving can figure it out. Nor, I think, can any amount of human despair seal it off. That is almost as big a problem as the other, you know. Along with the people who believe it is their job to guard the door on God's behalf, there are others who will not go anywhere near it. They never even try the handle because they are so sure it is locked.

We will all be surprised, Jesus says. Some are last who will be first and some are first who will be last, but that does not excuse any of us from trying the door. It is important that we strive to go through it, even though our striving itself will not win us anything. It will simply teach us what we need to know. Some who are used to walking through open doors may find that this one requires more of them. And some who have spent their lives peering through darkened windows on tiptoe may find that the door has been open all along. God alone knows what we need. So I am glad it is God who is in charge of the door, the God who knows us all by heart.

Meanwhile, I think it is a good idea to keep the doors of the church open to all people. Let's just get everyone inside that we can, and leave decisions about the other door, the narrow one, to God. I think we can trust God to sort us all out, and to love us better than we love ourselves.

Twenty-seven

Why the Boss Said No

~

Jesus put before them another parable: "The kingdom of heaven
may be compared to someone who sowed good seed in his field:
but while everybody was asleep, an enemy came and sowed weeds
among the wheat, and then went away."

WITH THE NEXT MILLENNIUM ON OUR DOORSTEP, global anxiety seems to be running pretty high. Open any newspaper and you will get a full dose of how awful things are. No one I know is cheerful about the future. Whether the topic is the nation, the church, the economy, or the environment, consensus is that things are getting worse, not better. The whole creation is groaning, just like Saint Paul said, and the weeds seem to be crowding out the wheat.

Those of us who believe in God have a hard time explaining—to ourselves or to anyone else—why things are the way they are. Some of us fear an apocalypse and others hope for one. In the meantime, all of us wrestle with a world that is messier than we would like it to be.

The details may have changed since the Bible was written, but the dilemma remains the same: what should we do about this mess? What *can* we do, and why is it this way in the first place? If God really is in charge, then why isn't the world a beautiful sea of waving grain? Or at least the church—couldn't the church, at least, be a neat field of superior wheat?

According to Jesus, not even the kingdom of heaven is pure. It may have started out that way, but sometime during the night, while everyone else was sleeping, an enemy sneaked in and sowed weeds among the wheat—*Lolium tremulentum*, to be exact, better known as darnel, a nasty wheat look-alike with poisonous seeds and roots like nylon cord. If it is not separated from the wheat at some point or another, those seeds can get ground into the flour and make a loaf of bread that will give you a real bellyache.

Some commentaries dismiss the enemy business as Jesus' "conspiracy theory." They note that weeds do not require an agrarian terrorist to plant them. They grow all by themselves. But however the weeds get there, most of us have got them—not only in our yards but also in our lives: thorny people who were not part of the plan, who are not welcome, sucking up sunlight and water that were meant for good plants, not weeds. Some of them are just irritating, like poison ivy, but some of them are as deadly as nightshade. The question is, what to do about them?

"Do you want us to go and gather them?" the slaves ask their master. That is the commonsense solution. Pull them up, cast them out, cleanse the field. We have seen a lot of that lately—in Bosnia, in Northern Ireland, in the Middle East. Wherever people are busy trying to purify the field by hostile means, they are doing what the slaves wanted to do, only they are doing it without permission, because the Boss said no.

"No," he said, "for in gathering the weeds you would uproot the wheat along with them. Let both of them grow together until the harvest; and at harvest time I will tell the reapers, Collect the weeds first and bind them into bundles to be burned, but gather the wheat into my barn." This is a stunning statement, not least of all because it seems to advocate passivity in the face of evil. It

also seems to suggest that we can do more harm when we think
we are doing good than when we are doing nothing at all.

As far as I can tell, there are at least three reasons the Boss
gives for why he says no to those who want to neaten up the field.
The first is that they are not skillful enough to separate the good
from the bad. They cannot always tell the difference, for one thing.
They exterminate something that looks for all the world like a
weed but when they bend over to pick up the limp stalk, grains
of wheat fall out. Did you know that in one of the first crusades,
knights from western Europe blew through an Arab town on
their way to the Holy Land and killed everyone in sight? It was
not until later, when they turned the bodies over, that they found
crosses around most of their victims' necks. It never occurred to
them that Christians came in brown as well as white.

Another difficulty with separating the good from the bad is
that often their lives are intertwined. That is one of the ways darnel survives, in fact, by wrapping its roots around the roots of
the wheat so that you cannot yank up one without yanking up
the other. There is no plant surgeon alive who can extract the
poisonous seed without killing some innocent bystanders, and
according to the Boss it just is not worth it. Better to let them all
grow together until it is time to harvest.

A second reason to let the weeds grow is that they may turn
out to be useful in the end. In first-century Palestine, lumber and
coal were hard to come by. The best bet for heating and cooking
fuel was dried weeds or manure. By letting the weeds and the
wheat grow together, farmers had almost everything they needed
to make bread: the wheat for the flour and the weeds for the fire.
The only other thing they needed was a little patience, a little
tolerance of the temporary mess, until everything was put to good
use at the harvest.

For those of us living in the time before the harvest, that

patience can be hard to come by, but the weeds may still be useful in ways that surpass our understanding. I am thinking of the people who have been setting fire to churches lately—a real bunch of weeds if there ever were any—but I am also thinking of the incredible public response to their poison, with black and white churches coming together like never before to express their solidarity with one another.

Sometimes the weeds wake the wheat up and remind them who they are. Sometimes, when the field gets very, very messy, the search for the Sower becomes a necessity, not a luxury, and good seeds that once toasted in the sun taking everything for granted remember that surviving as wheat is going to take some effort.

Only *how* shall the wheat survive? By spending all their time attacking the weeds or by devoting the same amount of time to being wheat? The third reason I think the Boss says no to yanking the weeds is that the wheat run the risk of turning into weeds themselves. It is one of the trickiest things weeds do, to get the wheat so riled up and defensive that they start acting like weeds themselves—full of prickles, full of poison—good guys who turn into bad guys trying to put the bad guys out of business.

The Boss has warned us about that before:

> You have heard that it was said, "An eye for an eye and a tooth for a tooth." But I say to you, Do not resist an evildoer. . . . Love your enemies and pray for those who persecute you, so that you may be children of your Father in heaven; for he makes his sun rise on the evil and on the good, and sends rain on the righteous and the unrighteous. (Matthew 5:38–39, 44–45)

God allows a mixed field, in other words, and whether we like it, approve of it, understand it or not, God asks us to tolerate a mixed field too—both in the church and in the world—only this is not even remotely a call to passivity. It is, instead, a call to strenuous activity (as any of you who have tried to love your enemies lately already know). It is not easy being wheat, especially with so many weeds competing for the soil, but what the Boss seems to know is that the best and only real solution to evil is to bear good fruit.

Our job, in a mixed field, is not to give ourselves to the enemy by devoting all our energy to the destruction of the weeds, but to mind our own business, so to speak—our business being the reconciliation of the world to God through the practice of unshielded love. If we will give ourselves to that, God will take care of the rest—the harvest, the reapers, the fire—all of it. Our job is to be wheat, even in a messy field—to go on bearing witness to the one who planted us among those who seem to have been planted by someone else.

I once read a story about Pope John XXIII, one of God's great saints, who ended his lengthy prayers each night by saying to himself, "But who governs the church? You or the Holy Spirit? Very well, then, go to sleep, Angelo." As the next millennium approaches, following his example may be the only way any of us can sleep—by staying true to our roots and to the one who planted us, believing him when he tells us that the harvest is his.

Twenty-eight

Heaven at Hand

—

These twelve Jesus sent out with the following instructions:
"Go nowhere among the Gentiles, and enter no town of the
Samaritans, but go rather to the lost sheep of the house of Israel.
As you go, proclaim the good news, 'The kingdom of heaven has
come near.'"

MATTHEW 10:5–7

IN A WORLD THAT CAN BE HARD AND SCARY SOME-
times, it is tempting to think of the church as a hideout, the
place where those of us who know the secret password can gather
to celebrate our good fortune. As we repeat our favorite stories
and eat the food that has been prepared for us, it is tempting
to think of ourselves as consumers of God's love, chosen people
who have been given more good gifts than we can open at one
sitting: healing, forgiveness, restoration, resurrection. Then one
day the Holy Spirit comes knocking at the door, disturbing our
members-only meeting and reminding us that it is time to share.
We are not to be consumers after all, but providers of God's love,
authorized agents sent out to speak and act in Christ's name.

Next to the calling of the disciples, I expect that Matthew's
story about their sending forth is one of the most confrontational
stories in all the Bible. Can you imagine? There you are, perfectly
content to be a follower, when Jesus comes home all worn out

one day with his hair hanging in his face and his clothes ringed with sweat and dirt. He looks around at those of you who have been with him all along and says, "The harvest is plentiful, but the laborers are few. I need some help, and I'm nominating you." Then he holds his big hands out over your heads and says a prayer that travels down your backbone like a chill, giving you authority over demons, over disease—even over death—and when he has finished you open your eyes and look at each other to see if you can tell any difference. Next you take a deep breath to test whether anything has changed inside. Do you feel wiser, stronger, more capable? Nope. Just blessed, sort of. Just tingly and curious and, well, ready—not for anything in particular, just generally ready for whatever is next.

Then he starts calling names. "Jim and Bill, you take Baldwin. John and Nancy, Batesville. Bob and Gil, I'm thinking of Alto for you, and Hollywood for Mary and Anne. Ed and Roy to Clermont, Kathy and Carol to Mount Airy. Leave your wallets and pocketbooks here, everybody. You'll be traveling on foot—barefoot, actually—and you won't need a backpack. God will provide, and that will be easier for people to see if you don't carry all your own provisions with you. Here's what I need you to do: preach the kingdom, heal the sick, raise the dead, cleanse the outcasts, cast out demons. Boy, do I need a weekend off. You all have a great time. I can't wait to hear the stories you bring back. Now get out of here! Go, go, go!"

It does not happen exactly like that at church, but it happens all the same. At the end of every service, while the last word of the last hymn is still ringing in the air, a voice from the back of the church says, "Go forth!" "Go forth in the name of Christ!" "Go in peace to love and serve the Lord!" "Let us go forth into the world, rejoicing in the power of the Spirit!" Those are not words for consumers of God's love. Those are words for the providers.

Since we have been hearing this story about the sending of the disciples for so long now, we may take their job description for granted. In short, they were given exactly the same things to do that Jesus himself had been given to do, but it did not have to be that way. He could have pointed out that none of them was the son of God, after all. None of them had been born under a blinding star, or had angels sing hosannas over their cribs, or received exotic gifts from foreign dignitaries before they so much as cut a tooth.

He could have reminded them of all that and insisted that they remain his assistants—for their own safety, you understand, to avoid malpractice suits. He could have let them mix the mud when he healed blind people, or spray the Lysol when he cleansed lepers, or unwrap the bandages from those he had raised from the dead. He could have done that, but he did not. Instead, he transferred his ministry to them while he was still alive. He entrusted it to them. With no training and very little advice, he sent them out to heal wounds and restore outcasts and bring the dead back to life.

He also sent them out to preach the nearness of the kingdom, which was almost redundant. I doubt that those who were made whole by the disciples needed to be told that heaven was at hand. They knew that way down deep in their bones. They had already been to heaven in the presence of those who touched them in Christ's name.

Still, it was important for the disciples to say what they did and do what they said. Preaching the kingdom without doing anything about it is just politics, and good works without good news is no more than a temporary reprieve, but to proclaim the kingdom while acting it out—that is powerful, and that is what Jesus sent his friends out to do.

What keeps nagging at me, though, is the way he sent them

out—no money, no shoes, not even a walking stick. Why send them out with so much power and so few accessories? Personally, I think they might have had more impact if they had arrived in style like Willie Nelson's band, in a long, sleek bus with something catchy painted on the side, accompanied by their own driver, caterer, and publicist. That would have had some authority to it, some prestige appropriate to their task, but apparently that is not what Jesus wanted for them. The way Jesus set it up, they could not provide for others out of their own abundance: they could only provide for them out of their need.

There they were, vested with the authority to heal the sick and raise the dead, going barefoot from house to house, saying, "Excuse me, but may we stay with you? We can't pay you anything, I'm afraid, and we don't have anything to barter, but perhaps you could see your way clear to giving us a bowl of soup and a slice of bread?" There is tremendous paradox here. Are they beggars or miracle workers? And if they are miracle workers, then why must they depend on the kindness of strangers for a cup of water or a corner in which to sleep?

Not too long ago, a friend of mine told me about his time in Cambodia, where he learned about a Buddhist custom that seems to have something to do with this story. According to him, all seekers of the truth there spend at least a year of their lives as beggars. They go from village to village wearing nothing but a saffron robe and owning nothing but a begging bowl, asking perfect strangers to supply their most basic needs. After that year is over, they are free to return to their former ways of life, but none of them returns the same person.

What must it be like to own nothing, to have nothing but your own need, and to understand that the only thing you have to offer anyone else is what you yourself have been given? That whatever they give to you comes from what has been given to them? What must it be like not only to talk dependence on God but to live it everyday for a year, understanding that reliance on God equals reliance on the hospitality of others? That kind of knowledge could change a person for good.

After a year like that, you could hardly take your turn at the soup kitchen and hold yourself apart from the person on the other side of the counter. When you looked at her you would see yourself, or you would see God, but either way whatever you offered her would be offered not out of your abundance but out of your need. It would be offered out of your need to be related to her, your need to know about her life and to let her know about yours, your need to give her a portion of what has been given to you and to receive whatever she has to give you in return without thinking that makes you a hero.

It is simply what you do, when you know who you are and who you are working for, when you are sent out to proclaim the kingdom and to act it out with no money, no shoes, not even a walking stick. Because when it comes down to being a provider of God's love, there is really only one provider, who sends us out with nothing at all and with everything we need: healing, forgiveness, restoration, resurrection. Those are the only things we really have to share with the world, which is just as well, since they are the only things the world really needs.

Twenty-nine

Apocalyptic Figs

Then Jesus told them a parable: "Look at the fig tree and all the trees: as soon as they sprout leaves you can see for yourselves and know that summer is already near. So also, when you see these things taking place, you know that the kingdom of God is near."

LUKE 21:29–31

BE ON GUARD," JESUS SAYS TO HIS DISCIPLES DURING the last week of his life. "Be alert at all times." His advice tells us that he knows something about waiting, whether it is waiting for the ax to fall or for the baby to be born or for the kingdom to come. He knows how waiting can turn into a kind of solitary confinement, in which the senses are dulled and the mind wanders. He knows how easy it is to fall asleep while you are waiting, or to bite your fingernails bloody, because the one thing you are waiting for will not come and you cannot make it.

When you are waiting for something in particular, your brain has a way of phasing everything else out. Have you noticed that? If you are waiting for a certain car to pull into your driveway—it is two in the morning, say, and your seventeen-year-old son is not home yet—you are not going to pay a whole lot of attention to the sound of an airplane overhead or the hum of the refrigerator cutting on. Your ears, your entire being, are tuned to one frequency alone, namely, the clatter of his Ford Pinto, which has needed a tune-up for months. If someone tries to talk to you while you are waiting for that sound, you may pretend to listen, but only until—shhh!—you hear a car come down the road.

Scientists have devised a game that proves how hard it is for us to notice something when we are expecting something else. Here is how it goes. They sit you down at a table in front of an ordinary deck of cards and they flash six of them at you, asking you to identify them as fast as you can—nine of diamonds, three of hearts, jack of clubs—whoops! What was that one? Then they repeat the exercise, slowing it down a little so you can get the ones you missed the first time.

The third time is so slow that you think you must be an idiot because there is one card you simply cannot identify. You think you know what it is, but you are not sure, and it is not until the cards are all laid face up on the table in front of you that you can see what the problem is. The mystery card is a six of spades, only it is red, not black. The deck has been fixed. Someone has changed the rules, rules that prevented you from seeing what was there. You could not see a red spade because spades are supposed to be black.

Our expectations, however faithful, may prevent us from seeing what is there. I have often thought that the second coming would be wasted on me, because I have such a set notion about how it is supposed to be: the Son of Man, riding a white horse with wings right out of the clouds—touching down on the White House lawn, maybe, or the skating rink at Rockefeller Center. Only what if he comes as a Guatemalan Indian on a burro, or a Tibetan exile on a yak? What if he comes out of the housing projects of Richmond on a broken-down bicycle with dreadlocks down his back? Stranger things have happened, after all. "Is not this the carpenter, the son of Mary?" Red spades have always been hard to see.

"Look at the fig tree and all the trees," Jesus says. Never mind red spades. That is graduate-level work, and most of us are still in kindergarten. If we want to learn what God is up to, we can begin by attending to the world around us. There are parables happening on every street corner and clues to the kingdom in every square foot of earth, but most of us are not looking for them. That is what Jesus was getting at, I think, when he told people to look at the fig tree. They may not have done that for a while. They may have been focused on abstract things, like judgment or salvation, or on dramatic things, like earthquakes and plagues. By directing their attention to a sprouting tree, Jesus let them know that they did not have to work so hard, that God was speaking to them in the most ordinary events of their lives.

"No one sees a flower, not really," wrote the painter Georgia O'Keeffe. "To look at a flower takes time, like having a friend takes time." Everyday I hear people say, "I don't have time; I'm out of time." I say it myself, but the bald truth is that I have all the time there is. I do not have any more or less than Mother Teresa or my six-month-old nephew. I just make different decisions about how I will use it.

Have you heard about the new Life Clock? Invented by two Chicago men, it is shaped like a three-dimensional isosceles triangle. When you buy it, for about a hundred dollars, you program your age and gender into the memory and it starts counting down the hours, minutes, and seconds left in your life, assuming you will live to seventy-five if you are a man and eighty if you are a woman. To keep that from getting too depressing, the clock flashes inspirational messages every sixty seconds, things like "All resistance begins in the mind" or "Eat your vegetables."

Soon after the clock appeared, a newspaper reporter asked one of the inventors if he didn't think the clock was a pretty morbid invention. Not at all, the man said. "When you see that time is quantified, the quality of your life starts to increase," he said. His partner agreed with him. "We're born," he said, "they wind us up and say, 'Go and see what you can make of your life.'"

I think it is a pretty morbid invention, but I also know that time is passing for those of us who are waiting. Whether it passes quickly or slowly, time is all we have. The question is, how shall we use it? How shall we wait? Jesus' answer about looking at the fig tree sounds like an invitation to pay attention not only to what may happen in the future, but also to what is happening in front of us right now. It sounds like a clue that God may be reaching out to us through things we would not have thought of as "religious," even something as worldly as a fig tree in bloom.

Maybe you already know that the word "apocalypse" means "revelation," as in that moment when you are looking at something you have looked at half your life and suddenly you see it for the first time, whether it is the sun coming up through the trees like an iridescent peach or the sorrow in your neighbor's eyes or your own face looking back at you in the mirror. Revelation is the moment when you can see through, see into, see beyond what is going on to what is *really* going on—not because you are some kind of genius but because God decided to let you, and you happened to be paying attention at the time.

"Be on guard," Jesus said. "Be alert at all times." Not so you will know when to grab your crash helmet and head for the basement, but so you will know when the kingdom is near. So you will not miss God when God comes. "Stand up and raise your heads, because your redemption is drawing near."

There are all kinds of ways to wait, even when it is the worst you are waiting for. A friend of mine was eight years old when the Germans bombed London in 1940. She lived in the heart of town with her grandparents, her cousin Bettine, and a big English sheepdog named Blitz, who went with the family to their sandbagged garage when the air raid sirens sounded. They shared the shelter with a Swedish couple who had a daughter about the same age, and what my friend remembers is what fun they had.

"We saw things in those sandbags no one else saw," she said. "We hunted for gold in them and we found it. Then we hid it again. Sometimes we found goblins and fairies too. There was a whole world down there that the adults couldn't see. They sat up on their beds reading their books and when we got too loud they'd say, 'Shhh, we can't hear the bombs.'

"Then we would listen too and if the explosions were nearby we would get scared, only the Swedish girl taught us what to do. 'Lie on your back and cross your arms over your chest,' she said, 'and God will protect you.' After the bombs stopped we would howl with laughter. We would sneak outside and look up at the sky—the beautiful sky where all that ugliness came from—until some warden came along with his flashlight and shooed us back inside. Then Blitz would get in bed with us and Grandmother would tell us such wonderful stories. I tell you, we had an awfully good time!"

There are all kinds of ways to wait, apparently. There is the tense, dread-filled waiting of those whose hope is gone. There is the resigned waiting of those for whom a spade is always a spade. There is even a kind of compulsive waiting, in which one collects signs of the end like souvenir spoons. Get the whole set and—poof!—the rapture comes.

The problem with all of these, as far as I can tell, is that they assume God operates by the same rules we do and will never slip a wild card into the deck. Only what if God's hand is all wild cards, including some greens and blues? The only way to wait for a God like that is to look, to be on guard, to be alert at all times, so that we do not miss the revelations we are being offered everyday of our lives—streetcorner parables and apocalyptic fig trees, gold in the sandbags and children howling with laughter at bombs dropping from the sky, the beautiful sky.

How shall we wait? As wide awake as we know how. As fully alive as we can be, not because we have to but because we can, thanks to the one who has died, who is risen, who will come again—and again, and again, and again.